D0999633

N

# FOR THIS WE FOUGHT

# THE TWENTIETH CENTURY FUND

## TRUSTEES

| | |
|---|---|
| A. A. BERLE, JR. | MORRIS E. LEEDS |
| FRANCIS BIDDLE | ROBERT S. LYND |
| BRUCE BLIVEN | JAMES G. MCDONALD |
| PERCY S. BROWN | WILLIAM I. MYERS |
| HENRY S. DENNISON | CHARLES P. TAFT |
| JOHN H. FAHEY | HARRISON TWEED |
| OSWALD W. KNAUTH | W. W. WAYMACK |

## OFFICERS

JOHN H. FAHEY, *President*

HENRY S. DENNISON, *Chairman, Executive Committee*

MORRIS E. LEEDS, *Treasurer*

EVANS CLARK, *Executive Director*

J. FREDERIC DEWHURST, *Economist*

# WHEN THE WAR ENDS

# FOR THIS
# WE FOUGHT

*Guide lines to America's future*

*as reported to*

THE TWENTIETH CENTURY FUND

*by*

## STUART CHASE

NEW YORK

THE TWENTIETH CENTURY FUND

1946

COPYRIGHT 1946 BY THE TWENTIETH CENTURY FUND, INC.

*(W)*
*no other no.*
*Nov. '46*

MANUFACTURED IN THE UNITED STATES OF AMERICA
COMPOSITION BY THE ACADEMY PRESS, NEW YORK
PRESSWORK BY E. L. HILDRETH & CO., BRATTLEBORO, VERMONT

338.973

C38

# FOREWORD

38644 THIS VOLUME is the sixth and last of a series of reports written for the Twentieth Century Fund by Stuart Chase to give the general reader a dynamic understanding of the great issues of postwar America. Planned before Pearl Harbor, the first four volumes in the series appeared while the war was on and while most of the nation's energies were being poured into the conflict. But even then the Fund believed that a clearer definition of goals for the peace would be a tonic for morale in war.

Then the war ended. We were catapulted into the postwar world with unexpected suddenness. The problems Mr. Chase set himself to explore in advance were no longer projections and predictions but headline actualities.

And now, eleven months from V-J Day, they are still with us—some of them more urgently than ever. Taken as a whole, this series of little volumes gives the general public a moving and exciting panorama of the whole range of grave questions the answers to which are the only passwords to lasting prosperity and peace.

The first volume of the series, *The Road We Are Traveling: 1914-1942*, was published in April 1942. In it Mr. Chase gave his colorful interpretation of the sweeping changes in our social and economic life which took place between the two world wars, and laid down a sort of base line for a preview of the future.

In the second book, *Goals for America: A Budget of Our Needs and Resources,* published in November 1942, Mr. Chase put into ringing words the needs of the American people which must be met to make a better world after the war and, using overall figures of the goods and services these needs demand, he argued that we have ample man power and resources to produce them.

In *Where's the Money Coming From?,* published in November 1943, Mr. Chase carried the discussion one step further. He maintained that, not only shall we have the man power and plant to meet these postwar demands, but we shall be able to finance the full employment of our human and material resources.

However, in the fourth book of the series, published in January 1945 — *Democracy Under Pressure* — Mr. Chase pointed out that the United States must be united in fact as well as in name if this high destiny is to be fulfilled. He portrayed the drift toward monopoly in business, agriculture and labor, which is preventing us from achieving the maximum volume of employment and production and he indicted the great pressure groups for threatening to divide the nation by placing their own selfish economic interests above those of the public.

In *Tomorrow's Trade,* number five in the series, Mr. Chase skillfully cut away with sharp-edged description and analysis the bewildering complexities of international trade, foreign exchange and overseas loans and investment to reveal the basic essentials of sound economic policy: America's need to accept a large volume of imports, to help break down the

barriers to the freer exchange of goods and services throughout the world and to finance recovery abroad.

In this final book, Mr. Chase has explored the larger national and international issues which all of us face—but
seen through the eyes of the veteran, returned from the
wars with new perspectives. Mr. Chase finds that all of us
want pretty much what the veteran wants and in the light of
our wartime accomplishments, he shows us some of the
ways in which we can reach our goals—in spite of the bar-
rage of difficulties through which we must struggle.

This series has been designed to provoke thought and to
stimulate discussion. Mr. Chase has been given entire freedom of authorship and he takes sole responsibility for all
the material in these books. However, in preparing the
manuscripts he has had the advantage of advice and criticism
from members of the Fund staff and a number of outside
consultants. But the opinions and conclusions expressed in
these books are those of Mr. Chase. The Trustees and Fund
staff take no position either for or against them.

This series is, of course, supplementary to the Fund's
regular program of economic research by qualified experts
and the formulation of economic policies by distinguished
non-partisan committees. Current projects include a major
survey of the foreign economic relations of the United States
with special emphasis on problems of foreign exchange,
loans and investments and commercial policy—under the
directorship of Norman Buchanan. The factual findings,
and a program of policies to be formulated by an authorita-
tive special committee on the basis of the research, are
scheduled for publication in 1946. Winfield W. Riefler is
Chairman of the Committee. International cartels, which are,

of course, interwoven with many other strands of our foreign economic relations, are being intensively studied in another current Fund survey. George W. Stocking and Myron W. Watkins are directing the research, and a special committee under the chairmanship of James M. Landis will formulate the program for action. The first volume resulting from this survey—*Cartels in Action*—a case study of cartel arrangements in seven leading areas of the world's economy, is scheduled for publication this fall.

In the field of financial and fiscal policy, which Mr. Chase explored in *Where's the Money Coming From?*, the Fund has recently published a volume giving the views of six leading professional experts. This volume, entitled *Financing American Prosperity: A Symposium of Economists*, contains contributions from the following authorities on the subject: B. M. Anderson, John Maurice Clark, Howard S. Ellis, Alvin H. Hansen, Sumner H. Slichter, and John H. Williams.

Another Fund survey now nearing completion under the direction of J. Frederic Dewhurst, the Fund's Economist, is designed to lay out base lines in each field of the American economy for dealing with its future problems. On the foundations of previous experience and of past and current trends the needs and demands of the American people for various kinds of goods and services are projected into the years 1950 and 1960 and are compared with the resources that will probably be available to meet them.

EVANS CLARK, *Executive Director*
*The Twentieth Century Fund*

330 WEST 42D STREET
NEW YORK 18, N.Y.
JULY 1946

# CONTENTS

# FOR THIS WE FOUGHT

# 1

# MEN IN NEW SUITS

J EFF IS A COMBAT veteran.
He was brought up by middle-class parents in a small
town near a big city. He was a blue-eyed, open-hearted boy,
chiefly interested in football and gliders. The Army caught
up with him just after he finished high school, and made a
navigator out of him. He was overseas for almost three years.

He moved from New Guinea to Guam to Leyte to
Okinawa. He flew his appointed missions, and a few more
for good measure, with all the tension, horror, exaltation
they brought. He was wounded by flak over Manila, but not
seriously. He was a hero for a while, though a pretty destructive one. Some of the great cities of the Orient will
never be the same since he passed over. He was promoted
and decorated, and made much of when he first got home.

Jeff is just old enough to vote. The rest of his life is before him. Yet how can it be anything but an anticlimax?
He has seen it all, from the starkest kind of death to the
stars at 20,000 feet. Just now the only job available is shipping clerk in a nearby mill. His father thinks he should take
it before some other hero gets it.

I am uneasy about Jeff. His life is as truly on the scales as
it was the night the flak came through the turret. He has

lost his open smile, and his eyes are darker, his face lined. Sometimes he looks sullen and trapped. Is this what he fought for, just to come back to pack metal parts in a shipping room? For a time the future of the country depended on his skill and courage, and that of boys like him.

Jeff may or may not be typical of the boys who have fought. I know several like him in my town. And there are many—perhaps more—who seem completely unscathed. They fought and suffered, but the war apparently has not changed them. Is this because they conceal the hurt, or because there is none? I do not know. A counsellor at the Bridgeport Servicemen's Center says that most of the men who come to him have not been hurt—but they are men now, he says, not the boys who went away in 1942.

If you talked to most of the chaps you'd find 'em rather apathetic and cynical about things in general—and just glad to be home again. They'd tell you they didn't expect anything very much except no more parades, comfortable living in Civvy Street, the wife and kids or the girl friend again—all that. That's what they'd say. But, you see, they hardly ever say what they're really thinking and feeling. . . . Underneath all that, most of these chaps really expect something wonderful to happen, a new sort of life.

And expect to have it handed 'em on a plate?

Yes, of course. They've been taught—or at least encouraged—to expect it that way. *You do the fighting, boys; we'll do the rest.* That's been the line, hasn't it? Well, they've done the fighting.

Thus a demobilized top sergeant talks to a London newspaper editor in J. B. Priestley's book, *Three Men in New Suits.* It seems to me that Mr. Priestley looks deep into the heart of the veteran, whether from London or Connecticut. They're all a bit cynical on top, but underneath they are hoping for something wonderful. Perhaps they have helped to win the last great war on earth. Perhaps there are going to be decent jobs for everyone forever. Perhaps . . .

## Perhaps Not

Overheard at a veterans' housing inquiry in New York:[1]

"Look, we just got married a couple months ago and my wife has to sleep at the YWCA and me at the YMCA. What kind of marriage is that anyway?"

"Listen, mister, I don't want sympathy. I just want a place to live."

"They're all tough cases, all 2,000 of 'em, and all we got is 600 apartments. I can't understand why the state and the city didn't plan for this situation a long time ago. They must have known it was coming."

## Figures

American combat deaths in World War II will far exceed such losses in all our previous wars combined. They will be close to 325,000, or six times World War I.[2] The aggregate of combat deaths in all American wars up to the last was about 250,000. Army deaths in World War II will be 255,000 to 260,000; Navy deaths, including the Marines and the Coast Guard, 65,000 to 70,000. The Navy combat deaths alone are greater than all deaths in World War I. The deaths of the Army in the European Theatre were four times World War I, and as great as the combat deaths for both sides in the Civil War. . . . This gives us an inkling of what our veterans have faced. The war in the jungles must have been one of the most terrible experiences men were ever subjected to.

Many of our fighters never had a regular peacetime job.

1. R. G. Martin in *The New Republic,* December 10, 1945.
2. Bulletin of the Metropolitan Life Insurance Co., November 1945.

They were taken from school or college, or from the ranks of the unemployed. Of those who held real jobs before the war, the following analysis, covering 9,600,000 soldiers and sailors, shows what they were:[3]

|  | Per Cent |
|---|---|
| Selling and clerical service | 24.3 |
| Factory workers | 20.2 |
| Craftsmen, other than building trades[4] | 10.9 |
| Farmers | 10.1 |
| Transport and communication workers | 9.1 |
| Professional men | 8.1 |
| Laborers[4] | 6.6 |
| Building trades' craftsmen | 5.1 |
| Unknown | 5.6 |
| Total | 100.0 |

## Skills

The National Research Council finds that the Air Force and the Army have trained men in more new skills than the civilian world can hope to absorb. We shall have a great surplus of air pilots, mechanics, radar men, electronic operators, and others.

I saw a mechanic one day get his stepladder all set against one of the engine nacelles of a B-29, waiting for the pilot to switch off the engines so he could start getting at the insides to tune them up for the next trip. The pilot finally switched them off, and the propellers coasted round and round, slower and slower. This mechanic couldn't seem to wait. He put out a determined gloved hand and eased the enormous blades to a stop; then he went to work with his wrenches. Mechanics worked through the nights and days for 24 hours, and sometimes 36 hours, at a stretch, without a rest

3. Quoted in Report No. 121, March 1945, National Research Council.
4. Some of these may also be in factories.

and with only some gulped coffee and Spam sandwiches, until the planes took off again. Major General LeMay, of the 21st Bomber Command, directed all commanders to examine personally the exteriors of their planes two minutes before takeoff time, to make sure that no mechanics were still clinging to the undercarriage.[5]

There was no money reward, no profit incentive in this concentrated effort. These were youngsters working for their fighting team and their country. When will they work like this again?

### Psychophoto of the Combat Veteran

Here is a composite picture of the combat veteran, drawn for the National Research Council.[6] Even if he is not a casualty, his nervous system is conditioned to active response for any unexpected happening—such as a land mine exploding. He can make the "bodily changes which enable the human organism to prepare to handle any objects in the outside world which arouse fear, anger, hate or rage." The blood supply to the extremities increases, while adrenalin is shot into the blood stream. Any soldier whose metabolism cannot adapt this way is soon a casualty.

Civvy Street calls for different responses. It expects people to be patient when thwarted. Here is a recently demobilized veteran who throws an axe at a dog stealing his lunch. Maybe we'd all like to do this, but we don't if we are civilians. We yell at the dog. Here is another veteran who tried to take a night club apart because it did not hold his reservation for a table. These men "had not yet developed, ready for instant control, ways of handling such events appropriate to the new situations."

5. St. Clair McKelway in *New Yorker,* June 9, 1945.
6. Report No. 121.

The Research Council argues for a "period of decompression," to allow the "superbly conditioned nervous system of the returned soldier to adjust to its new rate of activity." Jeff probably should not take that job in the shipping room yet. He might have an accident; smash something up. Many soldiers are asking for three months' rest. They should have it. Nature may be speaking for them.

Unless the soldier gets some new outlets, frustration is inevitable. A period of recreation, of completely following one's own desires, may well be an important part of the total transition from military to civilian life. Idleness, however, will not help. The veteran should have *action*. Let him go fishing or hunting or skiing.

The pent-up resentment and hostility in returned soldiers is no new development, but has been observed after every war for centuries. It is due to the regimentation, the frustration of military life, to lowered self-control from combat fatigue, aggressive tendencies encouraged in battle, to a feeling of injustice at having to face mutilation while another makes $100 a week playing safe. The resentment, in short, is due to many causes—above all, to a sense of status lost. One is no longer a hero, but another guy in a new suit, unsupported by a social purpose, or by that tight social group, the Army. Air Force officers take it particularly hard. Many of them are so young that they will find it very difficult in the Universal Gadget Company to win the same respect, or even the same pay, which they got in the 21st Bomber Command. "The blow to self-esteem is great, and the psychological reaction correspondingly deep," says the Research Council.

Millions of men have left the services "with no clear or

realistic goal." They won the war, and that was all the goal they had. The tie with their parents has been greatly loosened. The tie with wife and children may have been changed. "The community of interest which existed before the war is likely to be sharply reduced." The feeling of comradeship, of risks and dangers shared with one's buddies, is mostly lost in peacetime.

This team work, the Council observes, is probably the most enduring of all the satisfactions of military life. Team leaders feel an augmented responsibility in war, where life and death hang on instant decisions. Once acquired, these skills of leadership are not easily laid aside. If a veteran officer finds no outlet for them in civilian life, trouble lies ahead for him, and for Civvy Street.

The Research Council, in this study under Dr. Elton Mayo, has explained a lot about Jeff, about all combat soldiers. It is nonsense to suppose that impressionable boys can go through such devastating experiences and come out unchanged. Most of them will be perfectly normal when they come out, but the definitions of what is normal at the front and on Civvy Street are not identical.

The above applies primarily to the veteran who has had fighting experience, or at least been bombed. About 20 per cent of the Army never left the United States during the war; another 25 per cent were either in inactive theatres abroad, or far to the rear. But all had combat training, and every man who entered the armed services after 1940 was uprooted.

For many veterans, says Charl Rhode, there will be only a transient groping to reach some kind of firm footing in the civilian world. For others it will be a difficult process. . . . Every veteran in his return to civilian life brings along with him a special psychology growing out of military experience and therefore not duplicated in civilian life. . . . Certainly not all will have problems, but there will be few who can pick up where they left off.[7]

What is being done to help the adjustment? Let us take a tour through one of the best Service Centers in the country.

7. Bulletin of Menninger Clinic, July 1945.

# 2

# SERVICE CENTER

THE BRIDGEPORT Advisory Service Center is on a hill above the Court House. The visitor can park in a dead end street, and then climb a long flight of steps to a big yellow frame house. It is the kind of house prosperous merchants used to build in the 90's, with high ceilings, a wide front porch, plenty of pillars, balconies, and dormer windows.

A pretty girl sits at the desk-switchboard near the door. Waiting in line are two sailors, a captain, a corporal with a cane, three men in new suits with service buttons in their lapels. She receives them smoothly. "Will you sit down, please? Miss Sicilian will see you in a few minutes . . . Go right up; Mr. Sarkin is waiting for you . . . Major Griggs says that Mr. Robertson at the Third National knows all about that . . . No, we don't find jobs for anyone directly, we try to find out what you want, what you can do, and then steer you to somebody who can really help. . . ."

The men file past the girl's desk in the bright winter sunlight. Then they go out again, or upstairs, or sit down with a magazine in the big front room. From time to time, the girl calls to one or another that the counsellor can see him now, or to go to the top floor for an aptitude test. . . .

The men in the room look relaxed, easy, unworried. They like the girl, and the place, and the advice they are getting. There is no runaround here.

What kind of questions do they ask? Here is a typical list:

Are there any good jobs around Hartford now?

How can I learn to be a union carpenter?

Can I finish my last grade of high school at night school somewhere? Can this come under the GI bill?

Where can I get some legal advice about a divorce? You see my wife . . .

Is there anything new to read about raising chickens?

Will they take my mother's house away from us?

How can I get a land grant in Alaska?

What do I need to get a job as a mail clerk?

What is the best engineering school? You see I learned a lot about radar . . .

### They Saw It Coming

Bridgeport, almost alone among the war boom towns, saw the landslide coming. America is a big country, and in the past people have thought it big enough to absorb shocks without doing anything much about them. Bridgeport, however, took a terrible beating after World War I, and learned from that experience. So, with the help of Governor Baldwin and some manufacturers with long memories, citizens got ready this time. If the country goes reeling into inflation or deflation, Bridgeport, of course, will go too. But so far as a community of 250,000 can control its own destiny in the atomic age, the controls appear to have been well set up.

Every considerable organization in town has a hand in the Center: labor unions, Service Clubs, banks, social agencies, lawyers, doctors, the Red Cross, the churches, the YMCA, the hospitals, the Chamber of Commerce, the

CED, the city government, the state government, the U.S. Employment Service. The Veterans Administration works closely with the Center.

Expenses are paid from the Community Chest. Veterans are sent from the Center to one of these organizations, usually to a specific individual, with a definite appointment for an interview. "You go and see Margaret Conners about that legal matter at her office at 3 o'clock. She'll be expecting you" . . . "Jim Forbes can tell you all about that filling station proposition. He invented filling stations."

*Ninety-two Per Cent*

The idea of the Center is that the community must adjust to a big change as well as the veteran. It is a two-way road. Otherwise it might become We against They. The town cannot lie low waiting for the veteran "to get over it," or else he may never get over it. The town must meet him half way.

The Bridgeport area contributed about 30,000 men and women to the armed services, one out of eight in the whole population. When I was first there in late 1945, a quarter of them had come back. Of that number, 92 per cent had appeared at the Center with some problem or other. By April 1946, two thirds, or 20,000, had been demobilized, and the 92 per cent still held. The Center people, indeed, were worrying about the other eight per cent: where were they? The Center expected to handle 80,000 requests in 1946, indicating that most of the men came back with additional problems. The grapevine is active all over town. "Worried, soldier? Better go up and see what the Center can do about it; on Golden Hill Street."

Counsellors advise on five main kinds of problems:

Aptitudes and employment.

Financial and legal problems, such as buying a house, starting a business, holding onto government insurance. (Eighty per cent of their clients do hold on, far above the U.S. average.)

Family and social problems, such as the frequent breakdowns of hasty war marriages.

Educational problems. Shall one take advantage of the GI Bill of Rights for finishing high school, going to college, training school?

Benefits handled specifically by the Veterans Administration, such as medical aid.

Thus any veteran with a problem stands a good chance of getting some real help from counsellors who draw on a rich fund of experience. A few war workers, whose jobs have been demobilized under them, also come to the Center for help.

## Financial Advice

Here is a boy with corporal's stripes coming up the steps with his mother. She is crying and he looks white and scared. Their house is going to be foreclosed, and neither has the faintest idea how to prevent it. Major Griggs, the top financial counsellor, relieves this situation in practically no time at all. He sends an appraiser to see the property and to check with the grand list. He finds the house is worth a good deal more than the mortgage. He phones "Bill" at the bank. Bill executes a new mortgage, pays off the old one and back taxes with the proceeds. There is still a good safe equity in the property. The boy and his mother now rate Major Griggs on a par with angels from heaven.

"Suppose the appraisal showed the house had no equity?" I asked.

"Well," said the Major, "we are not a charitable institution. We'd have given them the best advice in town, but she might have lost the house. There have been some lost which we couldn't help. We get the finest kind of cooperation from the banks. If there is a knothole to crawl through to save a boy's property, they'll find it. If there isn't, they'll sit down with him and spell out why, no matter how long it takes. He mustn't go out the door feeling the community is doing him out of his rights. . . . We try to take the pressures off, not put more on; to make the boy feel everyone in Bridgeport is behind him, not doublecrossing him."

"How about a veteran starting a new business?"

"Most of our time," says the Major grimly, "is devoted to persuading them *not* to start a business. They would be in the cleaners before six months. Either they haven't the capital, or the background, or the know-how, or they can't tell a ledger from a Pari-Mutuel ticket."

## Security

The Army has accustomed the boys to the counselling method, and most of them actually enjoy it. They are not shy or suspicious. This saves the Center a great deal of time.

"What do the boys want," I ask Dr. Hamrick, the Director, "if it isn't too soon to generalize?"

"All ranks want security," he said, "from colonels down —we haven't had any generals yet. They have stopped grousing about welders getting $150 a week in war plants. If there were ever any such welders they were fired after V-J Day. The men want enough to live on decently, and bring the children up in a decent place. Many are keen for civil service because of the tenure."

"This doesn't check with what the orators tell us about sturdy independence and the American way of life," I say.

"I can't help that. It's what the boys want, almost 100 per cent of them. And you can't very well call them Caspar Milquetoasts."

"No!" I say, thinking of the 80,000 lost at Okinawa.

Dr. Hamrick also confirms Elmo Roper's analysis. As a result of twelve years of polling experience, Mr. Roper says that the mass desire for employment and security are not two different things, but two sides of the same thing. The average American's concept of security is a broad one, he says, and includes not only the right to work continuously at good wages as a kind of cornerstone, but other things such as owning a little home or farm somewhere, money in the savings bank, life insurance, a good education for the youngsters.

*Business for Themselves*

The Army has been making the GI's decisions for a long time. Many find it hard to decide things for themselves when they first come out. . . . "Cripes, I don't just know what I want to do." Yet an abnormally large number think they want to go into business for themselves, where they must make *all* the decisions.

Of those who had jobs before the war, more than half do not want the old job back. Why? Some had fine jobs; some put in years learning a skilled occupation, like carpentry. There must be something wrong with an industrial civilization which makes so many people dislike their work. Those who were taught new skills in the services often want to continue. But sometimes they have lofty ideas about the pay. A man classified in the Army as an "aviation mechanic" may have confined his activities to pouring gas into the tank of a bomber.

Of those who want to go into business for themselves, a quarter hope to open a tavern! Major Griggs has to discourage them fast, for there are no more tavern licenses available in the Bridgeport area. Almost another quarter of the prospective entrepreneurs want to run a filling station. There is a little leeway here—but not much more. Before the war one of the nation's prime exhibits in excess capacity was filling stations. Then the boys line up for running laundries, shoe repair shops, chicken ranches, small factories. Many have as much as $2,000 saved up, and could borrow more on good propositions. But good propositions are rare. . . . "I got three juke boxes, see, and I thought if I could borrow some money for some new records, I might . . ."

Here is a boy who wants to run a trucking service between New York and Bridgeport. He is sure he can make good, but he does *not* know that there are no more ICC licenses available for the route. Another boy wants to operate a local trucking service which requires no ICC license. He has the route all picked out and his eye on a truck. But until the Major suggests it, he had not thought of interviewing the merchants along the route to make sure there was a real need for the service.

The veterans are not bitter when they come in the big front door. They are not bitter when they go out of it. But if the luck is against them out on Civvy Street, they turn bitter. No house to live in makes them bitter. The racketeers and confidence-men make them bitter. The Major has to work nights to keep ahead of the get-rich-quick fraternity. The worst racket is the attempt to unload restaurants and cafes which have served their wartime utility and are now doomed to decay through lack of customers. The proprietor tells the veteran that he has taken a great liking to him. Seeing who it is, he says, he will let the cafe go for a beggarly $10,000. The veteran is impressed—until he runs into the Major's machine-gun burst:

"How long have you known him, ten days?"

"Why does he want to sell out?"

"Is there a war plant nearby? How many are working there now?"

"Have you seen his income tax statement?"

The grapevine has pretty well disposed of the furniture racket in renting a house or apartment. The Me-First gentry who offer a home at OPA ceiling prices, *if* the tenant will buy $10 worth of broken down chairs for $500, are not doing so well in Bridgeport.

### Three Stages

Most of the men go through three stages. When they first get home they want to forget the war, to rest, to sleep late, relax. Nature is taking a hand, as we noted earlier. In due time, they wake up, often quite suddenly, and ask, Where am I personally? What am I going to do? Has the mob got ahead of me? This is the stage when they come to the Center. They want to find themselves.

The final stage is when they begin thinking about matters *beyond* their immediate personal interests. It does not hit everyone, and often it is only a mild case. But bull sessions begin, breaking out on the stairs, in the reading room. How about the atomic bomb? How about Russia—have we got to fight her? How about the full employment bill, UNO, China, wages, inflation, strikes?

The anti-strike reaction is very strong when the men first come in. Overseas they have read about strikes holding up the weapons they needed to keep from becoming a casualty. But the anger begins to evaporate when they are no longer in personal danger. With the first job it frequently disappears altogether; the men sign up with the union; many go on the picket line. Those savants who hold that the GI's are coming back to run the unions out of the republic had better take a hard look at Bridgeport.

## Crisis in Schools

Early reports from some overseas areas indicated that servicemen were not greatly interested in continuing their education after arriving home. The *Saturday Evening Post* ran an article implying that the GI Bill of Rights would not be much used for more schooling. Educators figured their services would be in a bear market.

Dr. Tyrus Hillway, then chief educational counsellor at the Bridgeport Center, torpedoed this idea with a set of figures which took my breath away. The educators are due, he said, not for a bear market, but for the worst bull market in U.S. history. Of all the men who had come to the Center up to November 1945, no less than *43 per cent* wanted a GI loan for more education. Half of this group wanted to go to college. Many, of course, were in college when drafted. Thirty-five per cent wanted to go to business or trade school, or take training on the job. The rest wanted to finish high school.

The problem was to find enough colleges, trade schools

and high schools to meet this demand. The first two were already filling up. As for regular high schools, men with combat service do not fit into them too well. Cases are on record where the teacher got his eye blacked. Most trade unions were very chary of receiving more apprentices; they said such vacancies as they had must be reserved for their own veterans.

At the University of Colorado in Boulder, an entirely different sort of community, 1,500 miles from Bridgeport, I met the same problem. The University had enrolled 800 demobilized servicemen; "the most conscientious group of students I ever had," said President Stearns. Less than a third of the servicemen had come back to Colorado, but you could not get another man into the University with a hand grenade. A desk? Yes. Faculty? Perhaps—though a little down-graded. But a place for a student to lay his head? Absolutely no!

By April 1946, with two thirds of Bridgeport's veterans back, the school problem was much worse. Connecticut colleges were crammed, the high schools not ready, the training schools running far behind demand. More than half—the local Veterans Administration estimates 60 per cent—of all returned veterans now wanted more education. Many will be disappointed. A similar log-jam faces the entire nation. All the larger and better known colleges have long waiting lines. In New York state 200,000 students are clamoring at the gates of a university plant which has never accommodated more than 100,000. The major bottleneck, as at Colorado, seems to be a place for the student to live. By the fall of 1946, says General Bradley, 750,000 veterans will be attending college and another 1,000,000 waiting to get in.[1]

Here the towering housing crisis meets the gathering school crisis. If veterans want houses to live in and schools to go to, as they say they do, they are likely to be disappointed. Their only chance will be to have Civvy Street move as fast to produce implements of peace as it once did to produce implements of war.

Bridgeport can bring the entire resources of the community to bear when one lone, lost GI is stumped by the problems of a world he never made. If there is an answer to his problem, the community, catalyzed by the Center, can find it. Veterans feel this spirit throughout the big gaunt house.

Is there a pattern here for lone, lost youngsters in the communities of the atomic age? Bridgeport may be discovering something far beyond the matter of postwar adjustment.

1. *The New York Times*, May 5, 1946. Speaking to American Council of Education.

# 3

# WHAT THE VETERANS WANT

Many civilians can tell you exactly what veterans want by an act of intuition in which they identify the veterans' desires with their own. Is there any more reliable evidence? Fortunately there is.

The Army and Navy have been polling servicemen in a big way. A vast fund of information about young America has been accumulated, and someday will be released, perhaps with far-reaching consequences. Never was there such a garden of guinea pigs! Much of the material is still confidential, but I can report on certain assorted job lots which ought to give us a pretty fair idea of what soldiers hope to find on Civvy Street.

One survey, before V-E Day, sampled the whole Army, both overseas and in camp in the U.S., about postwar plans. Some 23,000 men were interviewed, selected to represent a true cross section of the millions in the Army.

Eighty per cent wanted to return to the home town, but not necessarily to the old job. Only a third of those who had a job before the war wanted to go back to it; another third said "maybe." This checks with actual experience in Bridgeport. Seven per cent of the sample—representing about 500,000 of the whole Army—hoped to go into business for themselves. Their average capital, however, was totally inadequate, to say nothing of the ability of Little Business to absorb new recruits on any such scale. How many wanted to open taverns is not reported. Many a prospective entrepreneur will probably be discouraged on reaching home. Advisers will tell him, as in Bridgeport, that one cannot be a successful businessman just because he likes the idea. One must have both capital and managerial ability.

Ten per cent of the sample group wanted to go into farming. That adds up to 700,000 new postwar farmers, probably more than American agriculture, with its many new labor-saving devices, can efficiently employ. Certainly we do not want any more marginal farmers.

Five per cent definitely looked for a civilian job in government, with another five per cent "maybe." All soldiers were emphatic in their opinion that veterans should have first call on government work. A survey a year later, in the summer of 1945, showed eight per cent definitely wanting a government job, and 11 per cent "maybe."

About 25 per cent planned more education under the GI Bill of Rights, 7 per cent full time, 18 per cent part time —night school or training on the job. This is far below the Bridgeport figure of 43 per cent, but we must remember that Bridgeport is an urban area in New England, where the cultural tradition is supposed to be high.

## Airmen

Here is another survey of 8,500 men in the Army Air Corps.[1] A third are officers, the rest enlisted men. Many officers are getting $300 a month and more. Eighty per cent

1. Reported in *Fortune*, August 1945.

of the whole group were single when they entered the service; now half are married, and even more—two thirds of the group—have two or more dependents. Almost three quarters were working before the war. Their average length of military service is three and a half years.

Forty-four per cent have jobs lined up when they quit, but they do not like them very well—the old refrain. Many men hope to find better jobs. You cannot blame them. For example, here is a pilot with rank of captain, who has a newspaper route waiting for him; another captain who can go back to the packing room in a glass factory; a lieutenant who has the way all cleared to stack empty gas cylinders in a chemical company.

What kind of work do these airmen want? Of those who plan for jobs rather than school, 21 per cent want to start a business of their own—another old refrain. What kind of business? Garage, trucking, retail store, in that order. Twenty-two per cent would like to work for a large corporation, 11 per cent for a small concern. Fourteen per cent want a civilian job with the government, 12 per cent want to stay in military service, 5 per cent want a farm, and 5 per cent a professional career. The other 10 per cent are scattering.

A third of the officers would like to stay in the air force, but only 3 per cent of the enlisted men are so inclined. On this basis, we should soon have more generals than privates—like a comic opera army. Of the officers who want to leave, half hope to get into commercial aviation. This seems a sensible ambition, until one checks up on the field. In 1941, there were less than 400 commercial planes in operation on all American airlines. Uncle Sam trained more than 100,000 pilots. Thus, with even *ten times* the commercial field available after the war, skilled pilots would still outnumber the jobs ten to one!

Twenty per cent of the enlisted fliers want civilian jobs in government; 10 per cent of the officers. Both are higher ratios than for the Army as a whole. All surveys I have seen demand high priorities for veterans in government work. What will Senator Byrd and the economy bloc say to this? If there is one thing a Congressman is more loath to do than raise taxes, it is to oppose veterans.

### More Army Surveys

Another survey indicated that 85 per cent of the men in the Army were in favor of organizing veterans. A new organization was preferred to a 1919 model.

When asked if soldiers should be given first choice of jobs that are open, or whether equality with civilians should be the rule, 70 per cent were for soldier preference, 20 per cent for equality, 10 per cent undecided. Thunderclouds here!

One conclusion drawn from these surveys is that if unemployment is serious in the years ahead, veterans are likely to feel they have been discriminated against. They may organize into belligerent groups, and a strong hostility against civilians may develop. If, on the other hand, the labor market is good, veterans will feel they have been fairly treated. Thus the future depends not only on what the veteran is like, but on what the situation to which he returns is like. Furthermore, the poll takers say, veterans must not only get a job, they must get the *right* job—or there will be trouble.

This brings us back to Mr. Priestley and his men in new

suits, and we quote again: "Most of the chaps expect something wonderful to happen. And when it doesn't happen, the fun will begin . . . Once it strikes home to them that they're going to be disappointed, that their *secret* hopes—and the fact that they are secret is important—are coming to nothing, then our chaps won't merely threaten trouble, as the last lot did in the early twenties, they'll *make* it. Deep down they're getting impatient. And they've seen a lot more in this war than the other lot did in theirs."

"A lot more of what—fighting?"

"No, the world—and what goes on in it. Quislings, black markets, reactionaries ganging up, people's resistance movements . . . Quite an education in its way."

### Mr. Kiplinger's Four Hundred

The Kiplinger Washington Service released a summary of more than 400 letters from men at the fighting fronts in June 1945. Contributions came from generals down, but the majority were enlisted men. The chief points were:

We want to go home.

We don't think much of foreign parts.

Most of us want jobs, and are afraid we won't get them.

We don't want the old job back very much.

Strikes and strikers are so and so's—a rich vein of four-letter words was opened here.

We are worried about getting a house to live in. (Right on the nose, Soldier!)

We are pretty sore at racketeers in Miami and elsewhere who rob soldiers, at John L. Lewis and Caesar Petrillo, at civilians who grouse about gas rationing, at black marketeers, at advertisements in four colors puffing products for "doing their bit," at Hollywood war heroes, at commanding officers, at rules and regulations generally.

We want to do quite a lot of studying when we come home, and our favorite course is engineering.

We want a hard peace for Germany and Japan.

We are worried about the future peace of the world. "We are winning the war, but we aren't so sure about the peace." (On the nose again.)

We think of ourselves as civilians temporarily fighting for our community—like our pioneer forefathers who manned the stockades when the Indians attacked.

Sometimes, however, the Army has become a career. Officers in the Air Corps have had great responsibilities and relatively high pay—as noted earlier. One of them wrote to Mr. Kiplinger: "I've been scared plenty by flak and things, but I'm most scared when I think of going back to $37.50 per week."

### International

A poll of the Army, at home and abroad, before the war ended, showed large majorities for the following international goals:

The U.S. should join the United Nations.

The world should have an international police force.

The U.S. should sacrifice some of its sovereignty for world peace.

### The American Veterans Committee

One of the new organizations is the AVC, led by Charles G. Bolté. Its slogan is, believe it or not, Citizens First, Veterans Second. Starting with the Revolutionary heroes, our veterans' organizations have never been backward about climbing on the gravy train. Already many Congressmen are at work on a Great Big Bonus for the boys of World War II. The older veterans' organizations will probably be solidly behind it.

But young Mr. Bolté has a long head. It is a different world this time, and for two reasons. In the first place, the American economy is now so interdependent that no one large class can prosper while the rest of us are in the dumps. For better or for worse, we must go up or down together. In the second place, if the veterans get a bonus or other forms of gravy, they will have to pay for a good share of it themselves! There are so many of them this time that they will form, with their families, a third to a half of the whole working population, and the most active part of it for years to come. Thus they will be the taxpayers, who pay themselves the Great Big Bonus.

When one considers the general high mental and physical standard of the veteran, combined with the normal preferences they have in employment, it is not exaggerating to forecast that perhaps half of all the earned income of the U.S. will go to veterans. What does this mean? Simply that . . . veterans' benefits will be borne by veterans themselves.[2]

Leaders of the AVC have clearly seen this tail-swallowing act. They hope the AVC will have no part of it. But if they do not want bonuses, there are four things about which the members of this organization are very insistent:

1. A real peace, founded on an international organization with teeth in it.

2. Jobs—not only for veterans, but full employment for all Americans.

3. Social Security. Again for all Americans.

4. A strong voice by veterans in future policies of the United States.

### Summary of Veteran Wants

From these surveys and polls, a pretty definite pattern

2. Charles Hurd in his column, "The Veteran," *The New York Times,* October 7, 1945.

emerges. Every veteran is different, but there are certain mass desires which Civvy Street will do well to respect.

The outstanding desire is for a good job, carrying security of tenure as part of it. Not fancy wages, but living wages for the family.

Veterans should have preference when jobs are limited, especially in government work.

A surprisingly large number of veterans do not want the old job back. They are restless, on the march for something better or more exciting.

A substantial minority wants to start in business for themselves. A majority of this minority seems to be ill prepared for the role of entrepreneur.

A large minority wants to continue education, full time, or part time, under the GI Bill of Rights. (In Bridgeport it is now a full majority of all veterans who have come back.)

Married veterans want homes to live in—not pup tents in Central Park, or a cot each in the YMCA and the YWCA. They may be rioting for this desire before these words are in print. There have been some housing riots already in Britain.

Veterans like civil service jobs because of the security of tenure, but they do not like signing up again in the armed services. Some officers in the Air Corps, however, will be glad to stay in the Army.

Most veterans don't want to be treated as a class apart. Probably they will want their own veterans' organizations in due course.

A large majority wants a world organization, a world police force, and is prepared to sacrifice some sovereignty for an enduring peace.

Unemployment is the major worry, greater in veterans' minds than the fear of World War III. When safe and sound citizens in Civvy Street scoff at the idea of full employment, calling it a "fetish," and incompatible with a free society, they should remember that millions of combat-trained young men do not agree with them.

In August 1945, General William C. Menninger, Chief

of the Army psychiatric work, told a Senate committee: "Positive assurance of employment to veterans when they become civilians is the best way of preventing medically discharged soldiers from becoming confirmed invalids . . . The assurance of sustained employment opportunities is therefore of the utmost importance to the mental health of the nation."

Thus psychiatrists, along with most lay observers, agree with the veterans. Mass unemployment is the primary curse and scourge of the modern economic world. There will be no peace on the domestic front until it is permanently vanquished.

# 4

# WHAT THE PEOPLE WANT

W<small>E HAVE GAINED</small> some idea of what the veterans want. What do the rest of us want? Elmo Roper, after years of testing public opinion, came to this conclusion: "The thing most demanded for our country by most people, of all economic levels, and in all walks of life, is *continuity of employment.* The specter of unemployment of the early 1930's must, they say, never be repeated again."[1]

Only a tiny minority, continued Mr. Roper, would like to see a form of society which failed to reward hard workers more than loafers. Nevertheless, "full employment is one of the things on the 'must' list of most Americans. If our present leaders cannot find a way of providing it, the people will seek and get new leaders who will."

Let us glance at a few of the polls which support this conclusion.

In October 1943, Dr. George Gallup asked the American people what they thought the biggest postwar problem would be. Far out in front as the major problem was *unemployment,* with 58 per cent of the people naming it. Next came *peace,* with 13 per cent; next *finance and debt,* with 11 per cent.

1. *Survey Graphic,* May 1943.

Two years later, but still in the pre-atomic days, the Roper organization asked Americans to grade postwar problems. Here are the results:[2]

*Major problems:* unemployment, Russian relations, the German settlement, the Japanese settlement.

*Intermediate problems:* labor unions, race frictions, the UNO, veterans.

*Minor problems:* inflation, relations with England, with France, with China.

The people not only want continuity of employment, they want the federal government to underwrite it. Poll after poll establishes this point. Our fellow citizens are voting in effect for a "compensatory economy," though they may not know the term. Governor Dewey's definition of a compensatory system is as good as the next man's: "If at any time there are not sufficient jobs in private employment to go around, then government can and must create additional job opportunities."[3]

In another study,[4] made in 1942, Mr. Roper asked a sample of the American people: *"Which of these things do you think the federal government should or should not collect enough taxes to provide for after the war?"* Observe that this question is barbed by pricking the tax-paying nerve. But the people overcame their anti-tax reflex with these surprising results:

2. *Fortune,* August 1945.
3. Speech in San Francisco, September 21, 1944.
4. *Survey Graphic,* May 1943.

|  | Should | Should Not | Don't Know |
|---|---|---|---|
|  | Per Cent | | |
| Jobs for everyone able and willing to work but who can't get a job in private employment | 67.7 | 25.2 | 7.1 |
| Compensation insurance for everyone unable to find work until he can find work | 57.8 | 34.4 | 7.8 |
| An old age pension for every citizen over 65 | 73.8 | 21.7 | 4.5 |
| Medical care for everyone who needs it | 74.3 | 21.0 | 4.7 |

The largest majority in this particular poll—more than 3 to 1—is for medical care for everyone. The American people want good health. Yet as I write, the lobby of the American Medical Association, under the able leadership of Dr. Morris Fishbein, is fighting the Wagner health bill with no holds barred.

The compensatory idea is approved by more than two thirds of the people, with 7 per cent undecided. It is interesting to compare prosperous people with poor people here. Both groups are in favor of government stepping in to insure full employment, but the prosperous majority is 52.2 per cent, while the lower brackets' is 78.6 per cent! The tax barb in the question seems to have caught prosperous citizens more sharply.

Private industry, said Mr. Roper looking at his poll results, should provide the jobs if possible, but wherever it cannot do so "it is, according to our people, the firm and fixed obligation of government to see that every man who cannot obtain a job in private industry is provided with work." The so-called Murray full employment bill (S.380) was designed as a first step in meeting this obligation. It remains to be seen whether the bill as finally watered down and amended will have any real effect.

A poll by the National Opinion Research Center at the University of Denver in 1943 reported 85 per cent in favor of an extension of the present social security law to include health insurance. A *Fortune* poll in August 1945 showed 77 per cent in favor of the extension of social security to everyone, including farm workers, domestic workers, and the self-employed.

### Factory Workers

In 1945, the Office of Public Opinion Research of Princeton took a poll of factory workers. Only half of them had heard of Senator Murray's full employment bill. When it was briefly explained to them, however, 74 per cent favored and 12 per cent opposed it. When asked who would do the most to solve job problems after the war, 47 per cent said the government, 24 per cent said management, and 14 per cent said labor leaders. The rest were undecided.

Asked what union members should try to achieve after the war, most of the factory workers thought the major objective was the protection of war wage rates; next came a system of annual wages. Here we find the security idea strongly emphasized. Workers do not want to slip back; they want to go forward to a guaranteed yearly income. They also believe, by a considerable majority, that labor leaders and managers should fight less and cooperate more. It would be nice if leaders and managers saw it that way.

Sixty-one per cent of factory workers think that if a veteran had a job before the war, he should get it back, even if it means displacing a civilian with greater seniority rights.

But if the soldier never had a job, the civilian should *not* be displaced. Many veterans think otherwise.

## International

In June 1944, Dr. Gallup reported the "vast majority of U.S. citizens vote in favor of cooperation with other nations in enforcing peace through some sort of world union after the war." Polls have shown heavy majorities for a world police force.

*Fortune*, a year later, reported 75 per cent of the American people for the United Nations. Sixty-six per cent said that the U.S. cannot prosper if other nations are depressed. Forty-three per cent voted to continue war taxes to help the people of liberated Europe; 42 per cent said no—a photo finish. The rest were undecided. J. S. Bruner[5] reported 92 per cent of Americans favoring the continuation of food rationing after the war, "if necessary to feed people in countries hard hit by war." As I write, Congress is in no mood to revive rationing.

## What They Want

By and large, the polls indicate that the rest of us want about the same things the veteran wants. First comes employment with security yoked to it. Second comes peace, founded on some kind of world organization. The atomic bomb has made the second desire more insistent, but I have not yet seen any poll results which put it ahead of full employment at home.

The demand for employment, as Mr. Roper points out, has one significant angle. The best form of security, the

5. *A Mandate from the People*, Duell, Sloan and Pearce, New York, 1944.

American people think, is the right to work continuously. They want the business cycle smoothed out. They are fed up with working in fits and starts as hitherto. This is hardly the expected reaction of a spoiled or pampered people. *We don't want handouts, we want regular work.*

### The People, Yes

Carl Sandburg once wrote a stirring book by this title. He said the people were mostly right—but of course he was a poet. William A. Lydgate, of the American Institute of Public Opinion, has written another book proving that Sandburg was right.[6] Mr. Lydgate quotes chapter and verse to show where the people are often way ahead of Congress, ahead of the President, and several light years ahead of the editorials in most newspapers. Again and again, the people leave the leaders of the people buried in a cloud of dust.

When an up-to-date pollster like Mr. Lydgate says "the people" he means all normal adults in the United States; only children and defectives are excluded. His interviewers are supposed to ask their questions of enough people in all walks of life, in all parts of the country, to give a reliable cross section of the entire population, including both sides of the tracks. If the pollsters can phrase their question so that people do not get their emotions stirred, then we can be reasonably sure that a sample will give the true reaction of the whole group. The cross section problem is said to be pretty well solved. The neutral wording problem is more difficult, but progress is being made.

### Unions, Taxes, Social Security

Rank and file trade unionists were queried on the matter

6. *What America Thinks*, Crowell, New York, 1944.

of public accounting for union funds. Labor leaders mostly consider such proposals a personal affront. Yet 71 per cent of union members, according to Mr. Lydgate, are in favor of it. Polls show that Americans are not against unions as such, but turn in crushing majorities against so-called "feather-bedding," against "make work" policies, against strikes in wartime, against wildcat and jurisdictional strikes.

After Pearl Harbor, the willingness of the people to accept heavy taxes went far beyond what politicians thought possible. The average American, says Mr. Lydgate, "is not out to soak the rich, is not the sort who wants to get all he can out of the government and give as little in return as possible." The main grievance of the man in the barrel is a tax form which requires two CPA's and a Philadelphia lawyer to fill out.

The people were strong for the Ruml plan months before Congress got around to a grudging compromise. No less than 82 per cent of taxpayers favored the withholding-at-source system, while politicians declared with owlish certainty that the public would never stand for it. Congressmen behaved like frightened geese, however, when Doctor Townsend turned his fierce old eye upon them. They supported the Townsend Plan in battalions, because they thought the people wanted it. The people had too much sense to want $200 a month which they, the people, had to pay for. Only 3.8 per cent of the U.S. public voted for the Townsend Plan in one of the Gallup polls!

Mr. Lydgate, like Mr. Roper, finds the man on the street dominated in recent years by the quest for two kinds of security: economic security for himself and his family; world security for the U.S. in the family of nations. The GOP attack on social security, in the 1936 campaign, defied this mass desire, and helped to make Mr. Landon one of our worst licked candidates. Those who sneer at "cradle to grave" proposals for increased economic security will probably never win a national election.

## Ideologies

In the fearful ideological battles which have recently raged between "planning" and "free enterprise," it is interesting to note, according to Mr. Lydgate, that only three adult Americans in ten seem to have a clear idea of what is meant by free enterprise. Many think of it as something invidious like "freedom to take advantage of labor," or "freedom to exploit people who know less than you do"; many told the interviewers they thought it was "something they give away"—probably in little cartons like samples of soap.

Politicians place inordinate faith in the power of campaign oratory. They think a rousing speech will change opinion, and get votes. *It almost never does.* President Roosevelt did not need to brave pneumonia in the fall of 1944. He could have stayed snugly beside the White House fire and not lost .001 per cent of his vote.

Propaganda tricks are not so powerful as touted either. While the Chicago *Tribune* shouted against President Roosevelt and his policies editorially, and slanted its news against him, the decline in his vote in the Chicago area from 1940 to 1944 was only 1.5 per cent, *less* than the total U.S. decline in the same period. Sound and fury getting nowhere! The people read the *Tribune* for the comics or the sports, and remained invulnerable to political propaganda.

*Events, Not Words*

The polls bring out one conclusion of great importance. *Public opinion is changed by events, not rhetoric.* After the banks began to snap in 1932, people changed their political ideas rapidly. They snowed Mr. Hoover under, and told Mr. Roosevelt to experiment as much as he pleased. After the fall of France in 1940, they changed their ideas about international relations with great rapidity. Following the event in Japan on August 6, 1945, their opinions may be taking another major shift. Perhaps the bomb on Hiroshima has made a world state possible sooner than anyone expected!

This is very cheerful news when all is said and done. Also it makes sound biological sense. If the mass of the people were swayed by every hurricane of political verbiage which came down the street, the human race would long since have become extinct. The fact that *homo sapiens* keeps going—however waveringly—shows that somebody, somewhere, has stored up a little wisdom.

38644

# 5

# THE·FIVE-YEAR·MIRACLE

Wᴏʀ ᴀʀᴇ ᴛʜᴇ ᴄʜᴀɴᴄᴇꜱ of
the veterans, and the rest of us, getting what we want?
Americans fought primarily to win the war; then, if the
polls are to be trusted, for work, security and peace in the
postwar world. We did not have much security in 1940, with
eight to ten million unemployed at home, and wars erupt-
ing all over the planet. Shall we get it by 1950?

Before the war the country was still in the backwash of
the great depression. The gross national product (value of
goods and services produced in a year) had pulled up almost to where it was in 1929, but there were nine million
more in the population to share it, and neither our man
power, our industrial plants, nor our farms were fully
utilized. We were drifting along, without much aim, the
pressure groups spitting venom at each other. Many people
thought that was the best democracy could do. Some thought
the dictators were doing better.

The war, reversing almost every trend, completely trans-
formed our domestic economy. Let us consider the pro-
ductive miracle, ignoring for the moment its destructive
result in the war zone, and the incalculable human losses
that occurred everywhere. The sheer volume of output sheds

a strong light on what Americans can or cannot hope for after the war.

The miracle started after the fall of France in June 1940, when President Roosevelt asked Congress for 50,000 airplanes to strengthen America's defenses in a dangerous world. Impossible, cried the wiseacres. We haven't the money, we haven't the plants, we haven't the materials. Yet by June 1945, five years later, Americans had actually produced 297,000 war planes, nearly 100,000 of them bombers.

*People*

Early in 1940, about 45 million Americans were at work on some kind of lucrative task although many were on part time. Mr. Roosevelt had made some progress, to be sure, but one third of the nation was still seriously depressed. By early 1945, 65 millions were working—including the armed services—harder than most of them had ever worked before. The average work week in manufacturing rose from 37 hours to 45 hours, while the output per man hour also increased.[1] Payrolls in factories leaped to three times the prewar total. The median family income in 1935-1936 was $1,075. By early 1945 it had risen to $2,600. It was hard to find an American family whose income was not well above the poverty line.

The ratio of women in the working population climbed from 25 to 35 per cent. It was found that women could perform effectively in 566 out of 623 war occupations; roughly ten out of every eleven. In the Weyerhauser lumber mills in the state of Washington, I saw formidable

---

1. Final report of J. A. Krug, War Production Board.

young women, armed with long pikes, steering great chunks of Douglas fir through live water channels to the circular saws.

America never had the class system of Europe or of Asia, but she had poor people, middle-class people, rich people. The war gave even this fluid class structure a tremendous churning. The sons of poor farmers and factory workers became officers in the Air Corps. The sons of millionaires were drafted to fight as privates in the Army. If they worked very hard, some became corporals. Junior League girls put on overalls to become expert spot welders in aircraft plants. Middle-class matrons, who had never done their own cooking, showed up on the graveyard shift in shops making parts for bomb sights. For five active years nobody knew who lived on which side of the tracks; or if they did, they did not give a damn. We were Americans fighting and working; a people devoted to peace, but terrible in war.

In this vast army of 20 million new fighters and workers, almost the population of two whole Canadas, were found the following groups:

1. Great numbers of young men, two or three million at least, who in 1940 were not in school and had no work but hung around the drug store and pool rooms, unwanted and listless.

2. Great numbers of Okies, Arkies and other migratory farmers, who had been tractored out by big-scale agriculture in the 1930's, or blown out by dust storms and erosion.

3. Perhaps 3,000,000 WPA workers, men and women.

4. The rest of the unemployed.

Although the point has not been stressed, this recruiting job of the fit, the near fit, and the 10 per cent fit, destroys in one vast controlled experiment the notion that people who are not working are the kind of people who will not work. The "bums and loafers" of 1940 turned into the fox-hole heroes, the flying fools, the dauntless naval crews, of 1944. The "scum of the earth" from the Dust Bowl built B-29's from San Diego to Seattle.

Presently, God help us, we shall again hear more talk about great blocks of our fellow citizens being a lot of bums. But in the face of this impressive demonstration, it can only remain talk—and pretty mean, low talk.[2] Mean-while, as Mr. Byrnes pointed out in his report as Director of Reconversion, the expansion of the working population from 45 to 65 million "poses the basic postwar problem."

### Things

In the five miraculous years, the volume of manufactur-ing trebled, and the output of raw materials rose 60 per cent. We made 76,000 ships, 315,000 pieces of field artillery, 165,000 naval guns, 86,000 tanks, and 2,400,000 war trucks and half tracks. Of the ships, 64,000 were landing craft, 6,500 were battleships, cruisers, destroyers and other naval vessels, 5,500 were cargo ships, to a total tonnage of 60 million—three times the British merchant fleet which led the world in 1939!

Before the war we moved the equivalent of 600 billion tons of freight one mile in a year. By 1943 we had jacked it up to a trillion. The number of passenger-miles on the railroads was quadrupled, from 25 billion to 98 billion in a year. The government built 1,300 up-to-the-minute fac-

2. From an editorial in the *Tulsa World,* January 1946: "The ideal of idleness has taken too great a hold upon this country. . . . It is more fashion-able to loaf than work. . . . It seems we want government jobs for all vet-erans . . ." and so forth and so on. This editorial writer, after sleeping for six years, has not skipped a beat since 1940.

tories, some of them half a mile long, like Willow Run. Near Knoxville, to use cheap TVA power, a whole city was built, and for a time 40,000 people lived there producing a mysterious product. On August 6, 1945, we found out what they had been making.

Now comes one of the most extraordinary miracles of all. So furious was our rate of work that we produced *both* guns and butter—to use the familiar symbols of a war economy. Before Pearl Harbor, most of the experts had said that America must choose. This was natural, because Germany, Britain, France, Italy, Russia, had chosen. America proceeded to turn out guns to the misty totals just recited, yet in 1944 its food output was great enough to keep its armies and allies well supplied, *and to give every citizen, on the average, 7 per cent more food than in the 1935-1939 period!*

Chairman Krug of the WPB summarized the "butter" situation in these words in his final report: "We had almost as much clothing—the textile squeeze did not come until 1945—as much food, as large a volume of services, and more miscellaneous goods, than before the war." The shortages for consumers were in durable goods like automobiles, in houses and house furnishings, in medical care with so many doctors overseas, in gasoline, in special foods like meat and sugar.

In 1940, we spent $66 billion for consumer goods and services; in 1944 $98 billion. True, goods cost somewhat more in 1944, but the two figures show clearly enough that, considering the whole picture, the war did not hurt American consumers very much. In all other countries, except possibly Canada, consumers fell far behind their prewar standards. Even Germans, with the loot of Europe, did not catch up.

In his careful studies of American wartime productivity in *Fortune,* Charles R. Walker concludes that after 50 per cent of total output had been delivered to the government "on top of that achievement, and in spite of red points and ration cards, the American standard of living kept close to the highest levels ever reached."[3] The war output which was superimposed on the civilian output dictated but did not displace it. In addition, Mr. Walker notes, $25 billion of new capital goods were produced during the war!

If somebody had stood by with a giant pair of scales, he might have found that America produced as much by weight in civilian goods as before the war, plus as much again in war goods—mass fabricated ships, tanks and planes. Gross national product rose from $97 billion in 1940 to $199 billion in 1944. Prices also rose. Perhaps the total tonnage was not doubled, but certainly the increase was massive and utterly unprecedented.

*Money*

Daniel W. Bell, Under Secretary of the Treasury, has provided a financial summary of the war which reads like an astronomer's table.[4] From July 1, 1940 to July 1, 1945— the five-year period we have been discussing—$833 billion cascaded around the dollar circuit—not far from a trillion smackeroos! The outgoing stream looks like this:

|  | In Billions |
|---|---|
| Individuals spent or saved | $428 |
| The federal government spent—mostly for war | 323 |
| Business firms spent or saved | 41 |
| Local governments spent or saved | 41 |
| Total | $833 |

3. January and February 1946.
4. *The New York Times,* November 25, 1945.

Turning to the income side of the account we reach the same total, as follows:

|  | In Billions |
|---|---|
| Individuals received in wages, salaries, dividends, etc. | $586 |
| The federal government received in taxes | 133 |
| Business firms retained in surplus and reserves | 65 |
| Local governments received in taxes | 49 |
| Total | $833 |

Now let us pick up the federal government story, and see how the war was financed.

|  | In Billions |
|---|---|
| The government paid out | $323 |
| It received in taxes | 133 |
| Leaving a deficit of | $190 |

During the five years only 41 per cent of the war cost was covered by taxes, leaving the government $190 billion in debt for the period. But by the laws of double-entry book-keeping, if the Treasury had a deficit of $190 billion, there must have been a surplus somewhere else in the economy to offset it. There was, and Mr. Bell shows us just where:

|  | In Billions |
|---|---|
| The savings of individuals and corporations increased by | $182 |
| The savings of local governments increased by | 8 |
| Total | $190 |

Thus, if we had taxed ourselves, and our corporations, and our local governments enough, and turned the proceeds over to the U.S. Treasury, we could have paid for the war as we fought it. While no net savings would have been made, neither would the federal debt have gone up by one thin dime. Taxes on this scale would have been far too heroic as political medicine, and probably as financial medicine too. But Mr. Bell makes it clear that the money to pay for the war *was generated in fighting the war*. The Treasury was financed as follows:

|  | In Billions |
|---|---|
| From non-bank investors, like you and me | $121 |
| From the commercial banks | 69 |
| Total | $190 |

You and I loaned our savings—dollars which we had already received from our war work or otherwise; dollars already in the circuit. The commercial banks, however, did not do this. They took the government bonds, and opened a deposit account for the Treasury to draw upon, thus, in effect, *creating $69 billion of new dollars, which had never been in the circuit.* The danger of inflation lay in these new hot dollars—and still lies there.

At the peak of the war effort, the government was spending $100 billion a year, $8 billion a month, $2 billion a week, $12 million an hour, $200,000 a minute, $3,333 a second. Tick! goes the equivalent of a sum which used to build a nice bungalow, or buy three good cars!

Contemplating this astronomical exhibit, some people feel their knees turning to water. Yet Mr. Bell's account makes it clear that every dollar spent for war goods also appeared in somebody's income account. A $50,000 fighting plane distributed, in its construction, exactly $50,000 in wages, salaries, dividends, interest, and other income to some person or business organization. It is this distribution,

still rattling around in our pockets, which makes many
people fear inflation today.

## Dynamo

One could go on documenting the war performance in-
definitely, but perhaps enough high lights have been given
to indicate the extent of the miracle. It is as though an
Olympian hand had reached down, grasped the American
people and shaken them into a fury of activity; whereupon
they proceeded to turn a chronic depression into feverish
prosperity, with strikes, featherbedding, monopoly, and
other delaying tactics at a minimum. They well-nigh doubled
their rate of output and changed its character drastically.
New machines were invented, improved, scrapped, re-
invented, re-improved, put into mass production. Assembly
lines appeared in mid-prairie and began to turn out cum-
brous monsters, never seen on earth, which at the touch of
a GI's finger could shoot, or aim, or hear, or, if necessary,
talk. In 1938 I wrote that tanks could not swim ashore. By
1944 amphibians were swimming up to the beaches, then
exploding into action all over the Pacific.

As Hanson Baldwin observes, it was quantity which won
the war, even more than quality.[5] "We possessed no such
overwhelming advantage in training for combat, in will-to-
fight, in leadership, in tactics, in the quality of our equipment. . . . But we could build an airfield or a pipe line in
a fraction of the time the enemy needed; and we could turn
out ten tanks to his one." In 1939 it was a truism that wars
had to be fought with whatever navy existed at the outbreak of war. Not this time! During the war we built a navy

5. *Foreign Affairs,* January 1946.

larger than all the 1939 fleets of the world combined! The Navy's pipeline, a floating-base system of supply, permitted a continuity of naval operations which five or six years ago was unimaginable. The logistical achievements of the naval war in the Pacific defy all comparison, says Mr. Baldwin; and there has been nothing in history even remotely approximating the shipbuilding achievement.

The story is endless. It can never be told in full, nor will the scars that went with it ever be fully erased from our planet. The point here is the profound transformation in American industry. Our workers supplied the material stuff to win a great war in the Atlantic, and another in the Pacific. They made a laughing-stock of the elders who had said in 1940: ". . . it will bankrupt the country" ". . . the people will never stand for it," ". . . we'll starve next winter," ". . . you can't do that."

The figures recited are not the record of economic ruin but of achievement. They show that prosperity follows activity. Imagine, if you can, what the achievement might have been had the goal been life rather than death; building new cities for the power age, rather than smashing existing cities to rubble! The conclusion here is not that chronic warfare is the cure for chronic depression, but a more hopeful one. People must have a *goal* to stir them to activity; something big to do, to make sacrifices for. Then their latent powers really come out.

The figures prove that high wages and high profits go together. Today, in 1946, in a wave of strikes, managers are striving to keep profits up by keeping wages down; labor leaders are striving to keep wages up by keeping profits down. Both sides are engaged in a hopeless task. In the power age, wages and profits tend to be functions of each other; they both go up—as in the war; or they both go down —as in the depression. The above figures also show a clear need for new fiscal inventions, so that we can pay as we go and not pile up so much internal debt.[6]

Perhaps the greatest industrial lesson of the war was the way workers turned out goods when they felt they were important partners in a great enterprise. Their performance made it clear that in peacetime a vast fund of human energy and cooperation has run to waste.

We learned in the war how to limit price inflation. In all other major wars, in all countries, prices have run off the map. In this war, not only here, but in Britain, Canada, Germany, Italy, Japan, they stayed on the map. (After controls were taken off in defeated countries, serious inflation of course soon developed.) How was it done? By taking surplus cash away from citizens in taxes and bond sales. By fixing prices and wages under such devices as the OPA, and the Little Steel Formula. By priorities for scarce raw materials, and by rationing of scarce consumer goods.

## Control Without Ownership

The war demonstrated that this furious collective output could be organized without using the socialist formula— public ownership of the means of production. The government went into the market, shouting orders and waving contracts. Businessmen took the orders, signed the contracts, and hired practically everybody who could still stand or see. Even some of the blind found employment. Though the

6. See *Financing Full Employment*, J. Philip Wernette, Harvard University Press, Cambridge, 1945, for a very pretty invention along this line.

government built 1,300 factories, it leased most of them to private companies. The government "took over" land for camp sites; it took over hotels in Florida; from time to time it took over Mr. Sewell Avery. But the fundamental policy was control without ownership, and its success is recorded for all to see.

The war economy was certainly not old style "capitalism," yet neither was it "socialism" in any accepted sense. It was something new in the world. If some of us could get the old labels out of our heads, we might see the world we live in more clearly. As Mr. Krug observes, the federal government guided, regulated, stimulated, and financed private enterprise in the national effort to achieve maximum production.

## War and Freedoms

Before the war many skeptics said that if we got into it we would lose our cherished freedoms, there would be no Congressional elections in 1942, democracy would disappear. What actually happened?

Elections proceeded as hitherto, even a bitterly fought Presidential election in 1944.

Free speech and free press continued, except for the withholding of military secrets. You could turn on the radio almost any evening to hear Upton Close roaring against the government, the President and our allies. You could buy the Chicago *Tribune* on any newsstand in its area, throughout the war.

Free assembly was everywhere permitted. Mr. Gerald L. K. Smith proceeded unmolested from one highly dubious gathering to another. Free worship was never interfered with.

Although in the Civil War, Lincoln was forced to suspend habeas corpus, the great principle came through World War II unscathed.

Freedom of movement within the country was not controlled,

though it was slowed down by heavy traffic. You might or might not find a place to stand in the baggage car.

Freedom to go into a store and buy what you had the money to pay for was limited by the rationing of certain scarce necessities. This is not undemocratic, however. Rationing lets rich and poor share alike in supplies which are limited. Without it, the big pocket-books would have grabbed it all.

Freedom to choose one's job was limited by the War Manpower Commission in certain tight areas, for certain periods. Most of the 55 million civilian workers never felt the hand of the WMC at all. (It was different in Britain.)

In *conscription,* however, millions of young men lost their freedom. Here "regimentation" became a grim condition.

So the wiseacres were once more confounded. Their picture of the war did not correspond to the facts as they developed. The war demanded a managed economy on a very broad scale. Yet it deprived citizens of no essential freedoms—except for the draft, and for the cruel segregation of a group of Japanese-Americans. Peering ahead down the *peacetime* years, it is hard to foresee any necessity of the economy being managed so tightly again.

Keeping the business cycle in line, providing full employment, spreading social security to all who need it, administering the debt, easing atomic energy into industry—none of these tasks will be easy. But in comparison with the physical achievements of making 297,000 airplanes from scratch, helping to beat Germany with one hand and Japan with the other, they are kindergarten work.

We return to the question which opened this chapter: Can the veteran, and the rest of us, get what we want?

The story just given clearly indicates that we in America can have anything we want in a material way, provided we want it badly enough to organize and discipline ourselves.

Furthermore, the story shows such vast dislocations from the "normal" economy of 1928, that any return is out of the question. Take the matter of the national debt as an example. In 1940 it was $43 billion; now it is about $270 billion, with carrying charges greater than total federal revenues in 1937.

It looks as if in one sense luck were on our side. Americans want work, according to the polls. The figures show that if we don't get work, the economy, even without our pushing, will break in two. Only full-scale activity, continuously maintained, can hold the economic system together now.

# 6
# LET DOWN

STRIKES CRIPPLE NATION'S PHONES
GM REJECTS FACT FINDING
CITY VIRTUALLY ISOLATED
GI's DEMONSTRATE IN MANILA
COAL AND RR WALKOUTS LOOM

These headlines in early 1946 are in sharp contrast to those of early 1945.

YANKS DRIVE INTO RUHR
BERLIN TOTTERING
JAP FLEET WIPED OUT
SUPER-CARRIER LAUNCHED

In the spring of 1945, Americans were driving two great wars forward to a victorious climax. It took all their energy, enthusiasm, will-power. Many citizens perished in the effort. Others complained, with or without justification, but nearly everybody knew where he was going, and where *we* were going. One hundred forty million of us were going in one direction. To what? To victory; to revenge for Pearl Harbor; to the obliteration of Hitler. That was enough.

Morale has been described in terms of a man's behavior

when he is working with his fellows for what he believes is a worth-while goal.[1] One cannot have this kind of morale by himself; it is a group phenomenon. One cannot have it without a goal in which to believe. From Pearl Harbor to V-J Day, American morale was high—yours, mine, the morale of everybody, except a few congenital misfits. The plane spotters, the wardens, the blood donors, all attested the fact.

But now victory has been won. Hiroshima and Nagasaki have paid for Pearl Harbor sixty times over in dead and mutilated. Hitler's charred bones lie somewhere under the ruins in Berlin. The goal has been achieved in terms of what most people thought the goal was.

What now? Americans do not know. They know what they hope for but not how to get it. Their great leader is dead and the urgent necessity ended. The coiled spring which kept them pressing as one unit has been released. Every man for himself now; every pressure group for itself. The current has been cut off from the magnet. The steel filings, which all pointed in one direction, now point in every direction.

### Bring the Boys Home

Six months after V-J Day, hardly a division in the Army, hardly a ship in the Navy, but had been so stripped of seasoned men that it could not fight a real battle. In February 1946, General Eisenhower turned in a very gloomy

---

1. Herbert Blumer, Professor of Sociology, University of Chicago, says: "Any people . . . may have high morale if the collective enterprise to which they are committed enlists completely their hopes, fervent wishes and aspirations." *American Society in Wartime,* University of Chicago Press, Chicago, 1943.

report on demobilization. Probably never in history had a victorious army disintegrated so fast. Yet it was not fast enough for Mom and Congress. "Faster," they cried, "bring the boys home faster." In Manila, Korea, Yokohama, Hawaii, Guam, Paris, Le Havre, Vienna, Frankfurt, the boys staged mass demonstrations to be brought home faster. Not only were they homesick, but many were afraid they would not find jobs, or houses to live in, or a college to go to, unless they were immediately released. Then there was another point, emphasized by Anne O'Hare McCormick:[2]

> More than they realize, they are depressed by the environment in which they live; the conquering hero cannot be happy long surrounded by ruin, want and hostility. More than they realize, they feel shut in with the conquered in a dull penal colony.

A private in Germany wrote Mrs. McCormick: "Why should we who won the war be expected to win the peace also?"

The demobilization score looked like this in early 1946:[3]

| | *(In Thousands)* | | |
| --- | --- | --- | --- |
| | *Army* | *Navy* | *Total* |
| Strength on V-E Day | 8,300 | 4,054 | 12,354 |
| Inductions since V-E Day | 800 | 123 | 923 |
| Total | 9,100 | 4,177 | 13,277 |
| Discharges since V-E Day | 5,000 | 1,542 | 6,542 |
| Strength on January 1, 1946 | 4,100 | 2,635 | 6,735 |
| Contemplated strength July 1, 1946 | 1,550 | 700 | 2,250 |

Thus in little more than a year, over ten million will be demobilized. One wonders how it could have been done much faster.

2. *The New York Times*, January 19, 1946.
3. *The New York Times*, January 13, 1946.

Many patriotic citizens protest. They say we fought for a more orderly world, to end war for all time, to make aggression impossible. Unless our soldiers are maintained in force to carry out these objectives abroad, the war, they say, will have been fought in vain. But the goals of the ordinary soldier were less far-reaching. He was fighting to win this war, to get it over with and get home, as the polls clearly show. This was enough of a goal to give him reasonably good morale. But when he had won the war, his morale collapsed. Nobody had sold him a loftier goal. Perhaps nobody could have done so.

### Recoil on Civvy Street

Civvy Street lost its morale along with the Army. Ordinary workers and farmers had not been sold a Utopian future either. Their goal disappeared with the cutbacks after V-J Day. National unity heaved and split. The pressure groups were out in the open again, bawling *Me First*. John L. Lewis closed down the coal mines to remind the country what a stout fellow he was. Caesar Petrillo, wrapping himself in his toga, forbade any foreign broadcasts of music. General Motors prepared to put the automobile union in its place; Alcoa got ready to recapture its airtight monopoly of aluminum. The cotton bloc, led by Senator Thomas, Oklahoma's gift to the Senate Agricultural Committee, prepared to bust the OPA if Mr. Bowles put a ceiling on raw cotton.

To unwind a total war economy is, of course, as much of a planned operation as to wind it up. American planning was good enough to build an army from 160,000 men to 10,000,000, practically over night, while doubling gross national product. But nobody in power wanted very much to be responsible for unwinding—with the exception perhaps of Mr. Bowles. President Truman had a program, but he was not expert in pushing it, while Congress treated it with disdain.

The National Association of Manufacturers demanded the removal of all price controls. *The New York Times* led a powerful press campaign to turn the whole economy over to the unfettered forces of free competition. The Sentinels were organized by businessmen in Detroit, pledged not only to end all war controls, but to repeal all social legislation since 1933! The mood of Civvy Street was to refuse responsibility for the changes which history had forced upon the country. Let nature take her course, and let us organize to get ours—this seemed to be the general idea.

### Strikes

As I write, two million organized workers have been on strike or threatening to strike. Westbrook Pegler can hardly keep up with them. Many angry people would like to make strikes illegal. President Truman's threat to draft workers when they strike against the government has evoked both applause and bitter resentment. Yet millions of fellow citizens cannot be moral delinquents. There must be a human cause for this outbreak of strikes.

To discern the causes one needs to look coolly at the situation and keep his temper, but that is not easy, especially if one is emotionally involved in the outcome. It is easier to think that some stubborn, greedy, and unreasonable persons on the other side are purposely thwarting us. Workers see managers of great corporations, bloated with war profits, standing in the way of their just rights. Managers see "communists" and "foreign agitators" standing in their way. Editors see wicked bureaucrats encouraging wicked labor leaders.

All these pictures are askew. Certainly there are willful egotists in the labor movement, as elsewhere in the community. There are some pretty mean chaps running corporations here and there. The strike crisis in 1946, however, is the product of the rank and file—far too many of them to be written off as undesirables. Look at the telephone girls, or the locomotive engineers. If they are wicked and greedy, so are we all.

What is troubling the workers? Chiefly fear for their security. They have vivid memories of the depression. "Am I going to lose my job again?" they wonder . . . "If the shutdown comes, can I stay in this town, or must I move again? Where do I find a house if I do move? What's going to happen to the kids?" Many families have already lost up to 50 per cent of their wartime take-home pay; a $3,000 family income has melted down to $1,500, while prices are moving higher.

A government survey of workers in Atlanta and Columbus showed that the jobs being offered in those cities to unemployed war workers represented a cut in take-home pay ranging from 34 to 53 per cent. Another survey in Trenton showed that men who had earned $60 in war work were being offered peacetime jobs at $40 and less.[4]

Workers were worried and uneasy for at least five reasons:
1. During the war they had been held to the Little Steel

---

4. Consumers Union Bulletin, December 8, 1945. Income payments to individuals held up better than expected on the whole, but many families suffered seriously.

Formula—wages to be not over 15 per cent more than in 1941. They had promised not to strike, and most workers kept the promise. Now that the war was over, their sense of fair play told them adjustments were in order. Many were tired after their long hours of overtime and wanted a breathing space. "I'd like to sleep for a month," a spinner told me in Manchester, right after the war. "It was always dark when I got up."

2. Unemployment had come for many war workers, especially in shipbuilding, aircraft manufacture, light metals, ordnance. Under the best of conditions these industries will be fortunate if they can employ one man in ten after reconversion.

3. Loss of overtime pay had been severe as hours dropped from 48 to 40 a week.

4. There was the loss of prestige and pay, due to down grading. A foreman in war industry went back to the bench after V-J Day.

5. Finally, there was the loss of prestige and pay in shifting from war to civilian tasks. A skilled welder for instance is asked to take a job as a dishwasher.

"At any level," says Ben Selekman, of the Harvard Business School, "this process of reducing standards is a thing of stresses and strains, of fears and frustrations."[5] Then he makes what seems to me a very wise observation: "The drive for full employment represents for the wage earner a direct promise of steady work, and so a chance for individual and family planning, something far more poignant than the national plans and employment budgets over which the policy makers dispute." How can one expect to buy a

5. *Harvard Business Review*, Winter 1946.

house, bring up a family, plan the children's education, when one never knows whether one will have a job at half the money next year, or no job at all?

The full employment bill was kicked around Congress for months. There was no economic security anywhere in sight *save in the workers' own organized efforts.* So they went on strike, or threatened to strike, while the GI's rioted in Manila and Frankfurt. This may all be temporary, a natural let-down after the tension of war. Perhaps, however, there is no cure until we get another goal to work for, and great leaders to help us achieve it.

*Managers*

If the worker is worried, so is the manager. The fact that corporate treasuries are bursting with cash does not help much. When, he asks, is the next crash coming? What has the war done to my business? Why is the whole world except America deserting the ideals of free enterprise? Why expand the plant if it is going to be vaporized by an atomic bomb?

Managers have been rendered jittery by one crisis after another ever since the stock market blew its top in 1929. Seventeen years is a long time to go without knowing where one is at; one gets no younger. The rest of the world has been in crisis since 1914, and shows no sign of calming down for years to come. Who would have dreamed that Russia would emerge from this war with the strongest army on earth, and making such frightening demands? Worrying about all this, managers find it hard to look objectively into the minds of their workers.

Since the New Deal was inaugurated they have watched

unions get stronger, and government interfere more with business affairs. Even foremen are now joining unions. A manager today gets crosseyed looking at his competitors, his union leaders, the OPA, the Treasury. Yet there is no escape. This is the way the world is in 1946. A manager must face unpleasant facts and handle them. Or he must quit.

Let us go back to the polls. Above all else veterans and workers want continuity of employment, a job they can count on. This desire is diametrically opposed to that of the business risk-taker and gambler who trades on the ups and downs of the business cycle. A great uncle of mine made four fortunes and lost three of them—one in '73, one in '93, one in 1907. If his way is the American way, as some allege, soldiers and workers are fed up with it. Perhaps managers of large corporations are fed up too. How can they plan their giant enterprises, or pay their "conventional dividends," with the economy going up and down like a roller coaster? Perhaps workers and managers are closer together than they imagine.

## Model Union

People wring their hands about the labor-management crisis. What is to be done? A great argument raged for a time about the demand of Walter Reuther to "see the books" of General Motors. Many believed that it was the equivalent of red revolution.

The Amalgamated Clothing Workers of America have been "seeing the books" for 25 years. They have not had a nationwide strike since 1921. The union knows the profit and loss condition of every employer. As a result the union steps gently when employers are operating on narrow margins. It becomes genuinely responsible, together with employers, for the health of the men's clothing industry. The union, furthermore, works out joint methods with management for increasing production and reducing costs. This lets the consumer in.

Why not? If a manufacturer is crowded to the wall by union demands, there are so many less jobs in the industry, and so many more members on the street to drain the union treasury. A smart labor leader does not price his men out of the job market.

In the depression, one of the largest clothing establishments was about to go into bankruptcy. The Amalgamated saved it by loaning the company a large sum and keeping it solvent. Again, why not? This is not philanthropy, but common sense and enlightened self-interest.

### Responsibility

The case of the Amalgamated Clothing Workers shows what managers and unions can do when real collective bargaining is practised. The industry is kept healthy, so far as both sides can bring it about, and the public also gets a break, in lower prices. The great question before the nation is how far genuine collective bargaining can spread. If it goes far enough, and fast enough, it can keep strikes at a minimum, and production high.

Americans must realize that the right to strike is one aspect of the right to leave the job if one so pleases. In spite of Westbrook Pegler, this is fundamental in a free society. To forbid strikes is to conscript labor; with state and police forcing a man to stay at his bench whether he wants to or not. It is a hallmark of totalitarian nations. William A. Leiserson, testifying before the Senate Committee on Education and Labor, said that passing a law to make strikes illegal will no more prevent them than Prohibition prevented drinking.[6] You cannot hold a man at his bench or at his desk, or even his switchboard, and still maintain the Bill of Rights.

The only way to stop strikes in a democracy is to make conditions so fair that people do not want to strike. In the Amalgamated, Sidney Hillman has educated his workers to the point where they do not want to strike—except in the direst emergency. They have the right, but they do not use it. They use their heads instead. Mr. Hillman and his staff, however, have been at it a long time. Unless many labor leaders and many managers show greater responsibility to the public than hitherto, collective bargaining will break down over large areas, and the federal government will have to go on intervening.

Dr. Alvin Johnson, a true friend of the workers, has thrown this challenge to their leaders:[7]

The sense of responsibility is far from permeating the entire labor movement. To many leaders of labor it looks very clever to tie up an industry just when the public interest may suffer the maximum damage. Tie up the port of New York while all America is yearning to get its boys home. . . . Tie it up when thousands of tons of food are awaiting shipment to the starving in Europe. Tie it up: labor proves its power! Labor has power indeed. But the American people are also possessed of power, and hate irresponsibility and tyranny.

6. *The New York Times*, January 17, 1946.
7. Bulletin of The New School, November 1945.

# 7

# WALK ALONG CIVVY STREET

THE VETERANS have been coming home, millions of them, into an economic system which is in the throes of reconversion, with no particular aim, and torn by labor-management strife. "We are concerned," said General Bradley of the Veterans Administration, "over the fact that estimates based on the latest census survey show about 1,000,000 veterans unemployed. In addition, over 1,500,000 more veterans not yet actively seeking work will enter the labor market shortly, and many of these will join the ranks of the unemployed."[1]

In early 1945, material munitions were being produced at the rate of $61 billion a year. By November 1945, the rate had fallen to $9 billion a year. For 1946, it is estimated at $3.5 billion. This is a terrific decline. When one adds the declines in government outlays for soldiers' pay, army camps, food, clothing, medical care, perhaps as much as $70 billion of orders will go whistling out of the market in 1946. This means unemployment for many, including some veterans, until civilian orders fill the gap. Strikes and lockouts help to keep the gap open.

On the other hand, we must not forget that at least $30

1. *The New York Times*, February 21, 1946.

billion of government orders will remain for 1946. If the
international situation becomes worse, the figure will rise.
This is five times the prewar outlay. It means a hard core
of employment maintained, whatever happens in Civvy
Street. There will probably be an average of three million
men in the armed services for the year, and they must be
supplied. In 1939 there were fewer than 500,000. From the
economic viewpoint, Army and Navy outlays are compar-
able to public works programs, underwriting employment.

Shipyards, aircraft factories, ordnance plants, were hit
the hardest after V-J Day. Output of metals, especially
aluminum and magnesium, was sharply curtailed. Fortunately, Mr. Baruch had worked out an excellent plan, which
Congress adopted, for cancelling contracts. Unfortunately
nobody had worked out excellent plans for the human be-
ings who were cancelled from these establishments, unless
the cheery reconversion reports of the CED could be called
plans.

At V-J Day or soon thereafter, the following war controls
were abolished:

| | |
|---|---|
| Man power controls | Output quotas |
| Gasoline rationing | Some price controls[2] |
| Fuel oil rationing | The Little Steel Wage Formula |
| All food rationing but sugar | Lend-Lease |

At the peak, an estimated 1,600,000 civilians had been
working in government war agencies, other than the Army
and Navy. As the controls were cut off, many of these people
were cancelled too, like the ship workers and the B-29
welders. Though tagged "bureaucrats," they had no social
security number to tide them over to another job.

2. When ceilings were removed from oranges the price promptly doubled.
The ceiling was put back.

*Inflation or Deflation?*

Unemployment was said to be less than expected by the turn of the year. It was impossible to count the unemployed, however, because of the confused aftermath of war. Millions of women, youngsters, oldsters, were leaving the labor market in theory, but sometimes changing their minds in practice. Millions of veterans were coming onto the market in theory, but often taking a rest in practice. Nobody, however statistically competent, could arrive at a reliable figure for total unemployment in early 1946. There was too much human nature mixed up in the computation. We could not know accurately about unemployment until the boys really showed up at Veterans' Centers and USES offices, and until Rosie the riveter made up her mind.

As I write, a kind of panic is developing over the imminent peril of a runaway price inflation. It is strongly reminiscent of ten years ago when many people were worried about the same thing. Well-to-do citizens remind one another of the terrible German inflation, when the savings of a lifetime would not buy a square meal. They point to the situation in Greece, where a 50 billion drachma note has the purchasing power of one prewar drachma. The stock market soars through an eight-year ceiling, despite 100 per cent margin requirements.

Without effective leadership and definite goals, it is hard to determine where prices for some goods might go. If ceilings are taken off a commodity before supply is within shooting distance of demand, prices will certainly go up for that commodity—as the price of oranges doubled. If the OPA law is upheld, prices should not rise very far. But there are many unknown variables. What will Congress do with the OPA? How fast can new production come in after retooling? Will people spend their savings, now at an all-time high? When will the strike wave recede?

These variables, and many others which might be mentioned, affect price inflation. There are, however, certain statements one can make about it—statements which have not been adequately considered in the current hysteria.

### Runaway Inflation Versus a Higher Price Level

One may distinguish at least two kinds of price inflation. One is the runaway printing press variety, now in operation in Greece, China, and elsewhere. The other is the 1920 variety in the United States where prices for many articles doubled over their 1916 levels. In 1921 they came crashing down.

The first can occur when a country is short of goods and raw materials, when its coal supply is cut off, or its cotton, lumber, iron, wool. In such an event people hurry to buy goods at any price as a hedge against the future depreciation of money. "In this kind of inflation," says E. M. H. Lloyd of UNRRA, "which may be likened to a forest fire threatening to consume a lifetime's savings and destroy the basis of orderly society, the rate of deterioration is the significant feature."[3] Mr. Lloyd calls it "hyper-inflation." In Greece in 1944 prices were rising by 100 per cent every three days. The drachmas you exchanged for a dollar would be worth three cents if you held them a fortnight; a tenth of a cent if you held them a month. I have here on my desk a Greek note, prettily engraved with the head of Minerva, for 100 billion drachma! I suppose it might buy a pencil, or perhaps a cup of flour.

3. *The Review of Economic Statistics,* November 1945.

"In the United States," says Mr. Lloyd, "there is no current or prospective inflation of this kind; and to call a rise of a few points in the cost of living per year 'inflation' is almost a misuse of the term." The U.S. cannot have hyperinflation because we have adequate raw materials, unbombed factories, a splendid distribution system, plenty of skilled workers. Those who nervously bid us "look at Greece" had better look more carefully at the physical plant of America —compared to poor, burnt-out Greece with her import-or-die economy.

Mr. Lloyd further points out the interesting fact that Egypt, Palestine, Syria and Iraq have had quite a price inflation while keeping their government budgets balanced. Allied armies have pumped money into the country, which, combined with severe reduction of imports, has led to an increase of wholesale prices of from four to eight times.

In his official report on reconversion, John W. Snyder said:[4] "With the exception of tin, rubber and a few other items, more of the raw stuff of manufacture is available right now for peacetime production than has ever before been used in the country in even peak peace years." Some durable goods are tight and will continue so for a while, many non-durables are in ample supply. If all controls are removed, says Mr. Snyder, sharp price increases are possible in some commodities, until the supply catches up. In most things it can catch up in a few weeks or months; in houses and motor cars it will take years. In nylon hosiery it is expected to take until early 1947.

Our potential supply has been considerably increased by the war. While other nations have had their factories, railroad terminals, harbors, bombed to smithereens, we added

4. *The New York Times,* October 2, 1945.

$20 billion of new plants. We doubled our inventory of machine tools. We trained millions of workers in new skills.

## The Historical Record

The United States has never had a runaway inflation in the Greek sense.[5] This is not because we are so wise, but because we happen to be a huge, integrated economy, with most major raw materials, both agricultural and industrial, in good supply at home, or readily available in North America.

The stock market has been roaring upward in early 1946, and many observers regard this as a sure sign of a runaway price inflation. Their memories are short. From 1922 to 1929 the stock market ascended grandly to the stratosphere, yet most commodity prices during the same period declined a little. We had a great boom with no price inflation at all. Why? Because the increased use of mass production techniques enormously speeded the output of goods. We had trouble with excess capacity during the 1920's, but none with inflation. The stock market was a thoroughly inaccurate guide.

Again in the depression, the facts disproved the theorists. When government deficits grew large due to relief spending, many bankers, economists and businessmen warned that inflation was inevitable. It never came. Why? Because the country had plenty of raw materials at fire-sale prices, plenty of idle plants and idle men, eager to go to work. If you look up the record you will find that the terror was widespread. Yet the inflationary scare turned out to be one of

5. A possible exception is the Confederate States in 1864 and 1865. The phrase "not worth a Continental" refers to the printing press inflation of the Revolution, before the Constitution helped to stabilize the currency.

those exercises in logic where one "proceeds from an un-warranted assumption to a foregone conclusion." Creditors are always on edge about inflation.

*We Can Have Both*

Even though a hyper-inflation is impossible, higher prices for some goods, until supply catches up with demand, are conceivable, and could seriously hurt a lot of people. There is no excuse, however, for allowing this to happen. We have a stream-lined, chromium-plated engine already in opera-tion which can stop any such rise, and we have first-rate engineers to direct it. To jettison the OPA as Congress now seems ready to do would be like throwing away the X-ray cameras, firing the hospital staff, and going back to bleed-ing patients.

Spotty inflation of this type is quite consistent with pools of unemployment here and there in the economy. California authorities expect at least 1,000,000 unemployed for some time to come. This is partly because so many ships and planes were made in California, partly because eastern in-terests hope to reduce the production of competing com-modities on the coast.

*Summary*

I think one can say this in summary and be reasonably sure of his ground. The chief danger along Civvy Street for the long swing is deflation. If nothing is done to pre-vent it, this deflation may occur on a scale to make 1932 look like Bingo night. We might have up to 20,000,000 un-employed. Before the crash, however, a boom in the stock market and in the prices of some scarce goods is quite possible, during which unemployment pools will remain but not spread. Gunnar Myrdahl, the Swedish economist, gives us six months to three years of spotty prosperity before the crash. The London *Economist* is not so optimistic. Mr. Baruch guesses five to seven years.

J. Philip Wernette, now President of the University of New Mexico, made this prediction:[6]

Immediately after the war there will be a brief re-stocking period, when business and employment will be fairly good. When the re-stocking stimulus has spent its force, however, the outlook for the decades ahead is for continuous, chronic world depression, broken by occasional periods of severe depression. That is what we may expect, *unless something is done to prevent it.*

## Those Savings

One of the unknown variables which make it difficult to foretell the immediate future is what people will do with their war savings. We have accumulated as individuals about $150 billion in the last six years, in cash, bank deposits and government bonds. This is regarded by the inflation school as so much financial TNT, ready to blow prices over the moon. I doubt this TNT quality.

In the first place, Americans have become inured to getting along without things. They may or may not spend lavishly on prewar models; they may wait for something really new. In the second place, having got ahead of the sheriff for once in their lives many people want to stay there. When the CED asked New York state farmers if they would buy durable goods out of their war savings, only 6 per cent said yes. The others wanted the goods right enough, but intended to buy them chiefly out of current income.

6. *Financing Full Employment,* Harvard University Press, Cambridge, 1945.

In the third place, the savings are pretty well concentrated in the higher brackets where people are looking more for investments than for consumer goods.

### The Crisis in Housing

The most likely place for price inflation is in housing. It may take supply five years to overhaul demand here, without some such spirited and planned action as we saw in building bombers. If government controls are entirely removed, contractors will naturally turn to projects where profits are greatest—in commercial structures, and in pseudo-Georgian jobs for junior executives at $20,000. So the folks who need houses the most, especially veterans coming back to their families, will get very few. The average veteran cannot afford to pay much over $5,000 for a house—following the rule of twice his income.

The social dynamite in housing may turn out to be more explosive, over the coming years, than in strikes. How long will a veteran consent to sleep in the YMCA while his wife sleeps in the YWCA? Men who have built gigantic bases from Australia to Japan do not see why they cannot have a roof over their heads at home. "It don't make a bit of sense," said a sergeant in the 341st Engineers to Richard Neuberger.[7] "Our outfit helped to build the Alcan Highway. We just got bulldozers and steam shovels and sailed into the job. Why not call on the 341st and have us build a few houses? We'd have a place to live in a few weeks." There is an alarming gap here between the tempo of construction the Army is used to, and the tempo the real estate gentlemen are used to.

7. In the *Nation,* January 19, 1946.

*Wilson Wyatt's Program*

To meet the housing crisis, President Truman appointed the young mayor of Louisville, Wilson Wyatt, as Housing Expediter. In due course, Mr. Wyatt produced a program calling for 2,700,000 dwelling units to be built before the end of 1947, primarily for veterans. The average cost was to be well under $10,000, and the program was to have priority over all other construction. If carried through in its entirety, it might come near to undoubling the doubled up veterans, but it would not end the ten million shacks and slum flats in which 50,000,000 Americans now live. There would be more demand for houses at the *end* than at the beginning of the program, from Americans generally. It was hoped that the Wagner-Ellender-Taft bill would help to take care of housing needs for the long swing—when Congress got around to passing it.

No sooner did Mr. Wyatt open his mouth than the real estate lobby jumped down his throat, crying "communism," and even if it isn't communism, "it can't be done." The real estate and construction gentlemen have never built houses for the two thirds of American families below the $2,500 a year income level. Most of us have always lived in second-hand to tenth-hand dwellings. The industry is thus some 70 years behind the automobile industry. It proposes to continue the methods of 1876 without shifting a rafter. Mr. Wyatt and the veterans have a fight on their hands almost as bitter as Anzio Beach.

Yet the public is solidly with them. Elmo Roper asked a sample of the American public about the Wyatt program.[8] Only 25 per cent were for taking ceiling prices off building

8. *New York Herald Tribune,* March 15, 1946.

materials. Eighty per cent favored government loans at low interest for medium-priced houses; 76 per cent were for priorities on materials for medium-priced houses.

And listen to this, Mr. Congressman! *Forty-eight per cent were in favor of the government going into the construction industry in a big way to build houses directly for the people!* Forty-two per cent were opposed, and the rest "didn't know."

Tanks we built, and ships, Ack-Ack guns, aluminum plants, and bases all over the Pacific. Lord! How we built them! But we have not yet learned how to build houses on the same formula. The building industry still operates in the pre-machine age. Touch it at any point, and a dozen pressure groups begin to hiss and spit. Yet no business is more hazardous, none closer to insolvency.

Only after a great roar from the veterans and from the rest of us, and after considerable assistance from government, are houses likely to roll out. Could this offer a goal to replace the goal we lost on V-J Day? It has a ringing challenge—Rebuild America!

### Back to Normalcy

Powerful interests in the American community, well represented in Congress in 1946, have an opposite goal. They fight every effort to plan reconversion, to build houses, to promote full employment, to hold down prices, extend social security, establish minimum wages, open up river valley developments. They are doing this because they believe, or hope, that the country is on its way back to "normalcy"—1928 model. Such hifalutin reforms, they hold, have no place in a sound, Coolidge environment.

Quite true, such proposals have no place there. What,

however, are the probabilities of recapturing the Coolidge era? That golden age ended, we should remember, with radio common at 540, and the biggest financial smash on record. There will be no real equilibrium, no "normal" period of any kind, until:

The atomic bomb is neutralized, and people can breathe easy again.

Relations between the United States and Russia are straightened out.

Europe finds some kind of pattern on which to keep body and soul together.

The Far East and the Near East do likewise.

Relations between the United States and Britain are clarified.

Labor, management, and government find a working arrangement for keeping strikes at a tolerable minimum.

People get houses to live in.

Methods for checking headlong depression and insuring full employment are put into practical operation.

The net national income is kept consistently at levels to service the national debt.

The machinery of the federal government is drastically remodelled to handle the problems of the atomic age. We could lose our democracy by sheer mechanical breakdown in Washington.

Fifteen million veterans and the rest of us find some real economic security.

The idea that now the war is over America can return to the piping times of Mayor Walker, Wall Street mergers, and flagpole sitters, is a dangerous illusion. It gets citizens off balance for the tangible events which are now hitting them and going to hit them. The world is passing through its greatest stress and change and turmoil since the break-up of the Roman Empire in the fifth century A.D.

# 8

# ATOMIC AGE—YEAR ONE

No man is an Iland, intire of it selfe; every man is a peece of the Continent, a part of the maine; if a Clod bee washed away by the Sea, Europe is the lesse, as well as if a Promontorie were . . . any mans death diminishes me, because I am involved in Mankinde; And therefore never send to know for whom the bell tolls; It tolls for thee. . . .

The prime movers of the Power Age have woven mankind far closer together than ever was the case when John Donne wrote his immortal lines, three centuries ago. Now the atomic bomb, and the promise—or threat—of atomic energy, have made all of us our brothers' keepers in a very special and terrible sense. Hitler, loose on the planet, could devastate half a continent. The next madman in control of a considerable nation can blow up the world.

Dr. Philip Morrison of the Los Alamos laboratory was sent to Hiroshima to investigate the effects of the first chain reaction employed against mankind. Testifying before the McMahon Committee in the Senate he said: "Of 300 registered physicians more than 260 were unable to aid the injured. Of 2,400 nurses, 1,800 were made casualties in a single instant. Not one hospital in the city was left in condition to shelter patients. . . . Debris filled the streets, and thousands of fires burned unchecked among the injured and dead."

Raymond Fosdick believes that in justifying Hiroshima on the grounds it shortened the war, and saved American lives, we made the winning of a war the sole criterion by which the moral legitimacy of weapons could be judged. "We Americans," he says, "started on its way a new method of volcanic destruction—started it with a reckless disregard of the future, leaving to our children and their children, the problem of how the bill will be met. . . ."[1]

I agree with Mr. Fosdick, but most Americans do not. A *Fortune* poll taken in December 1945, about three months after the two bombs were dropped, showed only one American in five ashamed of what we had done. Some thought more bombs should have been used.

Mankind is now confronted with a common enemy—the ignorance and confusion in man's own heart. Unless enough of us can realize that the bell tolls for *all* of us, some other race of animals may have to take over—if there is any living environment left to take.

Herbert Hoover, home from a world survey, finds 800 million people—more than a third of the population of the planet—threatened with hunger.[2] Americans, he says, are now eating about 2900 calories a day on the average. The minimum for health is 2200 calories. If the hungry abroad receive no more relief he estimates that:

300 million persons will be reduced to the 900 calory
                    level or below
300 million more will fall below 1500 calories

1. *The New York Times Magazine*, December 30, 1945.
2. *The New York Times*, May 18, 1946.

200 million more will fall below 2000 calories.

"As we descend this scale," says Mr. Hoover, "we move step by step from the stage of hunger to the stage of disease and epidemics, to the stage of public disorder, to the stage of starvation of all but the strongest, and finally, at less than 900 calories, we come to mass starvation."

This is a long, long way from the war goal of freedom from want.

### Europe

Winning the war has not turned out the way many people hoped it would. We have not got rid of totalitarianism and dictatorships, or spread democracy and the Bill of Rights over much additional territory so far. The principles of so-called free private enterprise are largely ignored except in the United States, where they receive perhaps more lip service than tangible action. Elections in Britain, France, Norway, even Switzerland, show a steady drift toward collectivism.

Worse than the failure of ideologies is the physical condition of Europe, including our friends and allies as well as our late enemies. Permanent peace and universal goodwill can hardly be built on a foundation of hunger, cold, and homelessness. The Nazis had most of Europe organized as an economic forcing machine. People who cooperated got food, coal, and supplies—not much, but enough to keep them going. The Allied invasion smashed that organization to flinders. So far nothing has been put in its place.

Some Senators see red at such statements. More handouts! they cry. Are the taxpayers never to be done with bailing out Europeans? This is not the issue. Is, or is not, the United States government responsible for its military acts, and its solemn promises? It was largely our bombers that demolished great areas in France, Belgium, Holland, as well as those in Germany. We killed our friends wholesale, along with our enemies. We left hardly a railway bridge standing in France. In the Atlantic Charter and elsewhere we pledged ourselves to help our allies build a new democratic Europe on the political ruins left by Hitler. This is not a matter of handouts, but of finishing what we started. If Europe gets no substantial cooperation from the West, her people must turn east to Moscow. Have the Senators thought of that?

Most Americans have not grown up politically. We think a war is like a football game or a presidential election—something to bet money on and to win. After we have won it is all over until the next war. But a military victory is not an end in itself. It is only a means to the real solution, which is always political.

According to the polls, people in Civvy Street believe we ought to back up our commitments in Europe and elsewhere with adequate military forces and funds.[3] *But they have little real interest in it.* Their real interest lies with the return of Jeff and his buddies, with strikes, nylons, the new Kaiser car, jobs, the housing shortage, and the supply of butter. We Americans had better face the fact that our forces of occupation are disintegrating to the point where they can back up very little. The Russian army is said to be in no such demoralized condition.

3. In March 1946 the Gallup Poll asked the question of all Americans: "Do you think it would be best for the future of this country if we took an active part in world affairs, or if we stayed out of world affairs?" The result: Stay in—72 per cent; Stay out—22 per cent; No opinion—6 per cent.

## Fiasco in Germany

Our policy in Germany is breaking down, both socially and economically. One reason is that it has failed to apply recent knowledge about psychology and economics. The broad approach has been along eighteenth-century lines.

There are about 70 million Germans, with the usual distribution from saints to sinners found in any large human group. They have, however, been wrapped up in one semantic package and treated as an *entity*. Our leaders and publicists seem to regard the Germans as a small boy who has been very bad and must be severely beaten so he won't do it again. After the birching in the woodshed, he will meditate on his misbehavior, turn over a new leaf, and ultimately be allowed back in the house.

By way of punishing the Germans for their sins it seems necessary to inflict hunger and disease and homelessness on 40 million women and children. This policy may satisfy our understandable feelings for revenge upon Hitler, but no reasonable person can expect it to "reform" the German population, or teach them any moral lesson, or help one iota toward the future peace of the world. On the contrary, it will make most Germans bitter and angry for the rest of their lives. The "bad boy" will certainly turn into a permanent juvenile delinquent on such a program.

In book 5 of this series,[4] I sketched the plan of E. H. Carr, the British international authority, for Germany after the war. It was to incorporate the Reich into a European Planning Authority, with rights like other European groups. There was no deliberate discrimination, no flogging in the

4. *Tomorrow's Trade.*

woodshed, no venting of revenge on innocent children. Professor Carr's idea was to make Germans less German; to melt down their Germanness.

Suppose Hitler had got the bomb first and won the war with it. It is not an inconceivable thesis. Let us follow it a little way. The Nazis proceed to make *us* see the error of our democratic methods. After due starvation and penance —300,000 die in New York City the first winter—we are to be allowed to carry on as a fourth-rate nation, with Nazi inspectors in every town hall, every factory, every store, every railroad station. All heavy industry is closed down. The contents of the Metropolitan Museum of Art are shipped to Germany—for safe keeping. . . . Would such treatment make us feel that our conquerors were wise and humane, and that we had better imitate them in the future? Or would it confirm every drop of bitter resentment?

*Economic Lunacy*

The procedure of the conquerors in respect to German industry seems equally primitive and unscientific. One would think the policy makers had never heard of a railroad, a coal mine, or a transmission line. A major characteristic of the power age is the *interdependence* of the people within its network. Men cease to be solely dependent on the land, as in handicraft societies, and a half or more—in Britain four fifths—become dependent on factories and inanimate energy. If the factories close down, most of the population must move or starve. This has been common knowledge for a generation.

The Pittsburgh of Europe was the Ruhr Valley in Germany. Here were the coal and iron and steel that maintained the consumer industries which kept alive, not only most Germans, but *most Western Europeans.* Not only were mines and factories concentrated in Germany, but also industrial know-how, and workers skilled in mass production. Our policy has been to force the power age culture of Germany, second only to that of northeastern America, back to the peasant culture of 1830. This meant driving the people within Germany's industrial network back a hundred years, including our allies in Denmark, Norway, Holland, Belgium, France and the Danube countries, and including neutral Sweden and Switzerland. How far would the standard of living in the United States fall if all industry in the northeast, within a line drawn from Chicago to Norfolk, were wiped out?

Let us follow the London *Economist* in this connection.[5] "It is not difficult to demonstrate the utter lunacy of the Allies' policy towards Germany." To compress 60 or 70 million persons into a territory roughly the size of Britain, and then de-industrialize them, can only lead to a disaster "almost as ruinous for Europe as for Germany." The wealth-producing machinery of Germany in late 1945 was almost completely idle, and Germany's neighbors were suffering. Iron production in the Ruhr was one per cent of 1944. "To the closed economy of Russia, to the super-productive economy of the United States, the decline of Europe cannot mean what it means to the unhappy Europeans."

## Japan

In Japan we are pursuing social and economic policies similar to those in Germany. Fortunately, there is, so far,

5. September 8, 1945.

only one administration instead of four. But Japan, like Germany, is being compressed into a rump state; Japan like Germany was the generator of a great power arc, with scores of millions dependent on her industrial output. By walling Japan up inside her home islands, we condemn not only great numbers of Japanese to economic extermination, but great numbers of our friends in the Far East as well. Think what would happen if the British people were walled up inside their home islands.

True, another nation may some day take over Japan's industrial role—perhaps China, perhaps Russia, perhaps ourselves. But how long will it require to make the transfer, and how many bells will toll in the meantime? And how will this industrial hiatus affect the revolution against white domination, now sweeping the Far East? True, we have the satisfaction of getting even for Pearl Harbor. Are we really aiding the unity of mankind?

God knows one wants no more irresponsible military aggression out of either Germany or Japan. To that specific end, would it not be safer to plan for 150 million Germans and Japanese, reasonably well-nourished and secure, than for half that number of gaunt victims cherishing undying resentment? Resentment by Germans against the injustices of Versailles was one of Hitler's two strongest cards. (The other was unemployment.) Versailles, however, was a patch of Utopia compared to what the Germans are getting now. The miners of the Ruhr are said to be so weak with hunger that they can dig little coal on 1,000 calories a day. Less coal means less fertilizer, furthermore, and less food at the next harvest. So the recovery of all Western Europe is lost in a vicious circle.

*Around the Map*

The international picture that follows our great victories is at no point a happy one. Troubles keep exploding around the Seven Seas. We have mentioned the revolt in Asia. Blood has flowed in 1946 in Java, Sumatra, Indo-China, Burma, India. In China, a civil war smoulders, and probably will continue—despite the wise hand of General Marshall—until Russia and the United States agree on a policy for China. This will not come tomorrow. Korea is seething, and we do not know clearly what is happening in Manchuria—probably something very unpleasant indeed.

The Near East is in ferment, with bloody riots and assassinations in Palestine and Egypt. The whole Arab world is marching—apparently toward some kind of regional autonomy. Yet right through the middle of the Arab territory run the vital pipe lines of the Anglo-American oil interests, and Britain's life line, via the Suez Canal, to the Far East. A worse political mess it is difficult to imagine.

Vigorous pressure is being exerted by Russia on Turkey and Persia, as I write. Indeed Russia, since her great military victories, has enormously enlarged her sphere of influence both in Europe and in Asia. Along all her borders, the pressure is unremitting. Wherever a soft spot is found, her troops and her political emissaries flow in. All of Eastern Europe has been inundated, and a large part of Germany.

Russia will not, I think, engage in major military action if she can possibly avoid it. Her war losses, both in men and industrial equipment, were monstrous. But the Kremlin will be ready by day or by night to seize any and all opportunities to strengthen the fatherland. The lesson of the "peace" following World War I has been learned well in

Russia. In 1919, five armies, led by British, French, American, and Japanese forces, invaded Russia from as many directions. Mention "Archangel" to a Russian even today and he jumps! Mention Denikin, Wrangel, Kornilov, and he grows white with anger. It is impossible to understand the diplomatic maneuverings of Russia in 1946, without reference to what happened in 1920.

Furthermore the United States has carved out vast new spheres of influence from Iceland to Central China, while Britain has widened her zone all over Africa, and from Central Europe to Southwest Asia.

> The reason world cooperation is not working any better is that the nations upon whose support its existence depends are acting as though it were everything when their interests could be served thereby, but at all other times they are pursuing policies of nationalism and spheres of influence as though they had never heard of UNO, much less joined it.[6]

As Ely Culbertson points out in his recent book, *Must We Fight Russia?*, it makes little difference how sincere are the promises of victorious allies to remain united; the promises are always broken. "What makes military alliances so valuable during a war is the cementing fear of the common enemy. . . . Once the danger of the common enemy is removed, the only real danger left is from one's allies. Each major victorious power naturally seeks to increase its own strength, and to prevent its allies, now potential rivals, from increasing theirs." The first rule of power politics is that no great state can entrust its future to the goodwill, promises or agreements of its actual or potential rivals.

In January 1946, the United Nations held its first meet-

6. *St. Louis Post Dispatch* editorial, March 21, 1946.

ing in London. For a little while, men of goodwill saw a ray of sunshine piercing the planetary gloom. Here might have been something beyond power politics. Then the light blacked out. The Persian delegation denounced Russia for military intervention in Azerbaijan, and demanded an investigation. The Russians then denounced British armed intervention in Greece and Java. Later, in New York, the Russian delegation marched out of the United Nations assembly on the Persian question.

The United Nations is a frail reed on which to rest our hopes of peace, and the control of nuclear fission. But it is all we have in this Year One of the Atomic Age. The hot breath of World War III—with temperatures exceeding those on the surface of the sun—seems to come nearer every day.

Did we fight for this?

# 9

# CAN WE GET WHAT WE WANT?

B OTH VETERANS AND CIVILIANS want economic security above everything else, as we have seen. A steady job, they say, is the biggest part of security. This means Americans do not want handouts; they want to work for what they get. Next to security, in the polls, comes a lasting peace.

Can Americans get what they want? In this chapter and in the next one we will explore the chances for economic security. In the last chapter, the chances for peace.

## More of the Same

Our analysis so far reveals a deep chasm between what people want, and what they are getting on the home front a year after V-E Day. Both veterans and civilians in too many cases are failing to find jobs at the pay they hoped for, or of the kind they desired. They are not getting enough houses to live in. Veterans are not getting enough school and college facilities. Congress has passed very little of the security legislation which the people, by large majorities, have said they want.

If the people wanted the moon, one could let them whistle for it. But they do not want the moon. They want something continued which is close to what they have had for the last five years—full employment, high levels of production, a pocket full of take-home pay for every one willing to remove his coat and go to work. More of the same seems to be what the people want, only at a somewhat lower tempo—say 40 hours a week instead of 50—and with some physical comforts to make up for wartime deprivations.

Is it Utopian to ask for what you've already had?

### Non-Material Wants

Many Americans got something else out of the war which they had long been hungry for. In addition to jobs and better incomes, they received a feeling of personal importance, of doing something worth while, of making sacrifices for something bigger than themselves. They got a sense of direction, and a definite goal. As the smoke cleared away from the burning hulks at Pearl Harbor, the goal looked exceedingly distant, and challenged American energy to its limits. How the whole nation rose to meet that challenge!

It has been said that our armed forces were not clear about war aims. For many boys, as we have noted earlier, the chief motive for fighting was to win the war and *stop* fighting. Yet what prodigies of endurance and valor they performed! What a rich mine of character and ability the country discovered—a mine which many leaders in business and government now propose to seal up until they decide they need the metal again.

War-workers, too, with motives more varied and less urgent than the serviceman's, showed unsuspected powers and qualities, called out by the first real opportunity many of them had ever had to show what was in them.

Few of us, soldier or civilian, liked either the idea or the practice of arms, but the war energized us. Today, we want no part of any more wars, especially atomic ones. All of us, however, would like to go on feeling our country needs us, feeling that we are going places in team work with our fellows. Sometimes I wonder if we could not make the best of both worlds by declaring a kind of perpetual war on the Martians!

*Sixty Million Jobs*

A good deal of the bitter argument about full employment has missed the main point. Output is not so important as the effect of a worthwhile job on the individual. The country could probably produce plenty to go around at something short of full employment. When atomic energy comes in, the man hours required to supply the essentials will take another dizzy drop. But to lay people off not only means that they cannot buy essential material goods; it also subjects them to a horrible kind of spiritual rot.

Man is an animal with a big brain, an opposed thumb, and other useful structures. Nature has decreed that he must use them or degenerate. Unless he is a glandular case, he *wants* to use them. He may not, however, as we saw in Bridgeport, want to use them at the old task. Production is of course important, but in these opening years of the atomic age, work—good, congenial work—is more important. It is better, I believe, to have people doing what they like to do, with a moderate output, than to have a great output at the cost of some millions of psychoneurotics. One major charge against the WPA projects was that they shifted the frustrations caused by idleness to frustrations caused by contemplating the futility of one's efforts. In the war, we were spared both.

## The Big Five

In *Goals for America,* book 2 of this series, we surveyed standard material wants—food, shelter, clothing, health services, educational facilities—calling them the Big Five. Without a steady flow of these essentials, a modern community cannot survive. Europe today is sliding back to the Neolithic Era for lack of them.

Americans lack only shelter, which is short and will be for some years. The other four can be provided in abundance any time we care to turn on the faucet. In 1944, with 12 million strong young men out of production, we turned out twice the gross national product of 1939.[1] Even while we contribute many supplies to the rest of the bombed, burned-out and hungry world, the material wants of America present no real problem. Our abundance can readily provide a minimum budget of health and decency for every family. In many special services and luxuries, of course, such as mink coats, scarcity will be the rule for a long time to come.

This potential abundance makes somewhat more hopeful the chances to get the jobs, wages, security, and goods we want. There is another large variable to consider, however, and that is the economic system itself. Output, employment, social security, are functions of the economic system. (Or if you shy at the word "system," call it a cluster of economic habits: banking habits, buying habits, saving habits, producing habits, and so on.)

---

1. It might not weigh twice as much. Gross national product represents the dollar value of all goods and services produced in a year.

Well, what kind of "system" are we going to have? What are the dealers offering in the new showroom of the postwar world? Let us have a look at the designs—and the price tags. Here are four standard models.

## Model A—A Mixed System, More or Less Hit and Miss

We can continue our prewar "mixed" system as heretofore, with government, business, labor unions, farm blocs, cooperative associations, non-profit enterprises, all making important economic decisions, and all struggling for power without much sense of direction. Under this arrangement, nobody is really responsible for anything until a serious emergency hits us. Then somebody in authority reacts—as in the "hundred days" in 1933, or after the fall of France in 1940. All of us react, indeed, and with great vitality. If you can recall the NRA parade in New York, you will remember how it rivalled the Lindbergh and Eisenhower celebrations for noise and enthusiasm.

## Model B—A Mixed System with Direction

We can continue our mixed economy, but not, however, as heretofore. Contrary to past performance, *we can really plan it with some intelligence and foresight,* as the Swedes have done it for many years in their "Middle Way." In this model a group of citizens in the Administration and Congress would be made continuously responsible for keeping the economy on a reasonably even keel. This is also known as a "compensatory economy."

Here is Governor Stassen's formula for Model B.[2]

I believe in free enterprise. The flaw which has shaken the con-

2. *American Magazine,* March 1946.

fidence of many in private enterprise has been the alternative between prosperity and depression, boom and bust. Some defeatists consider such swings inevitable. I disagree. These swings can be so moderated and smoothed out that their effects will be minor. Government can do this by a prepared and alert program, determined in advance, for using such instruments as taxes, credits and public works to maintain national stability.

## Model C—An Automatic Competitive System

Some Americans urge a return to the free competitive economy of the nineteenth century.[3] This would be quite a return, for free competition in the classical sense has been losing ground ever since the oil trust was organized in the 1870's.

## Model D—The Authoritarian State

Finally, we might conceivably be driven to an all out, planned, and centralized economy. Russia has one, Turkey another, but the American brand would certainly be quite different.

Historical forces are likely to select the model for us, but the immediate probabilities lie, I think, in A or B. Models C and D look improbable at this writing, and for the following reasons:

## Free Competition

In all the world outside the United States and Canada, the free enterprise ideal has ceased to have much vitality. Even here the competitive market has long since been infiltrated by business monopolies, labor unions, trade associa-

3. *The New York Times* editorial page, for example.

tion agreements, high tariffs, farm blocs, silver senators, patent pools, cartels, agricultural subsidies, joint labor and management restrictive agreements in the construction industry, and other pressure groups as we have seen.[4] Perhaps half of all goods sold to consumers before the war had been removed from the free, competitive market, to be manipulated by some vested interest.

Many people hope that the area of genuine competition can be somewhat enlarged by the promotion and protection of little business, venture capital, new enterprises. But one should not forget the 100 great corporations which got 80 per cent of all war contracts, or the fact that upwards of 500,000 small concerns went out of business during the war. One should observe in Bridgeport the appalling financial innocence of most veterans who want to go into business for themselves. Whatever the ideology in after-dinner speeches, the plain fact is, in the words of John M. Clarke: "Free private enterprise is getting less private and less free all the time."[5] Here is a run-of-the-mine sample:[6]

The Veterans Administration has long known that artificial legs which government orthopedic shops made for $62 were being sold by private firms for as much as $450. When the Administration tried to get lower prices through competitive bids, it often got identical bids from all members of the Association of Limb Manufacturers of America, which makes over 80 per cent of the nation's artificial limbs, and 90 per cent of the parts.

When this little arrangement came to light, the Department of Justice indicted the ALMA, 45 of its member firms, and 34 individuals, under the anti-trust laws.

4. *Democracy Under Pressure,* book 4 in this series, documents the decline in laissez faire in considerable detail.
5. *New Leader,* January 5, 1946.
6. *Time,* November 26, 1945.

Yet the ALMA, when the Veterans Administration tried to help the 17,000 servicemen who lost arms or legs in the war, had the effrontery to cry: "Government manufacture of artificial limbs will destroy free enterprise."

## The Authoritarian State

Whichever way you look at it, a return to the small, competitive society of the early 1870's is impossible. But if such a retreat is barred, so is an American version of the authoritarian state. The Office of Public Opinion Research of Princeton asked factory workers:[7]

Would you be for or against our government owning and controlling the banks, coal mines, electric companies and railroads in this country?
Against 62 per cent. For 27 per cent. No opinion 11 per cent.
Would you be for or against having our government own and control the factories in this country?
Against 74 per cent. For 17 per cent. No opinion 9 per cent.

Factory workers are supposed to be the proletariat, and so the most revolutionary of modern occupational groups. Imagine the negative majorities if farmers were asked these questions, or store clerks! Of course the poll does not distinguish between ownership and control, and many people who are opposed to government ownership, might favor a certain amount of control—as is now the case with banks, railroads, and power companies.

## Events Versus Ideologies

It takes a large, painful *event* to change public opinion, as we noted in Chapter 4. In a severe crisis, one could expect the above percentages to shift very rapidly, as they

7. *Factory,* January 1946.

did in 1932. If, for instance, Big Unions and Big Business got into a hopeless deadlock, cutting off the flow of steel, coal, freight cars, meat, electric power, telephone service, what not, the public would probably demand immediate government operation. Again, if Senator Bilbo and his friends succeed in wrecking Congress as a tribune of the people, the people might look around for another kind of tribunal.

Thus either the economy, or the political machinery, could break down so completely as to make an authoritarian state the only alternative to chaos in America. Otherwise, no amount of agitation, or propaganda, or indoctrination, or leaflets and speeches by organized fascists, communists or other revolutionaries, will bring it in. The polls of public opinion make that quite clear. *Only if no other methods are workable* can the majority of Americans be expected to submit to a completely planned economy.

### The Outlook for Model A

At the present writing, in mid 1946, America is operating a mixed economy on a hand-to-mouth basis. Each crisis is met as it comes along with what might be called "planning by ear." The WPA, the NRA and the RFC are good past examples. When something breaks loose, fix it by state action, but never anticipate anything breaking loose. The result is some badly-drawn legislation, always bitterly fought by pressure groups. Both sides in the fight make the fundamental assumption that it is an emergency measure only, soon to be rescinded as times return to normal.

Yet as we have seen, it is highly improbable that times will ever return to what used to be considered normal—

say the conditions of 1910, or 1926, or even 1937. America is in for one crisis after another for as long as we are likely to live. The atomic age calls for something more intelligent than hasty patchwork *after the crisis is upon us.* So far the call is unheeded by Congress and by the pressure groups.

President Truman has proposed a long-term economic program in line with Model B. He wants to get ready for these crises before they overwhelm the country. He has argued for it, made fireside talks for it, used the veto power, chided Congress. But Congress usually seems to be in neutral gear when not, indeed, in reverse.

Certain crises now looming on the horizon clearly call for some degree of planning, by ear or otherwise. The housing situation is rapidly developing into an explosive crisis, powered by angry veterans. Congress, after four or five million words in the *Congressional Record,* and more cries of "communism" from the real-estate gentlemen, can be expected to pass some bills which will help Wilson Wyatt to get part of what he wants. These measures will not solve the housing problem—far from it! But they may patch things up enough to keep people quiet for a little while. This is the way Model A works. Don't do anything until the heavens are falling.

Similarly, when strikes get out of hand, Congress rushes through a bill to punish strikers, but which only makes the fundamental labor problem worse.

Similarly, if later on the pools of unemployment rise until they flow into one large pool, Congress can be expected to forget all its pious resolutions about balancing the budget and to vote a few billions for relief and another WPA.

This is the trend now in June 1946. I do not say it will continue. Model A is terrifyingly obsolete. It cannot handle Russia. It cannot handle atomic energy. It cannot give Americans what they want. It may not reduce them to starvation, but it offers no security, no continuity of employment, no dependable flow of the Big Five, no goal, and no challenge to their energies.

Let us take a look at Model B.

# 10

# THE MIDDLE ROAD

Today in the first year of the atomic age the United States might be called a controlled economy with three chief engineers at the throttles:

> The Federal Government
> The Unions
> Big Business

Government is rated the most powerful by many people, but not by speakers in Union Square, who name Big Business. In the strike crisis of 1946, government and unions seemed to have lined up against Big Steel for 18½ cents an hour. But Big Steel got a price rise.

Not only are we a long way from a fluid, free enterprise economy where no organized groups are dominant, as pictured in the textbooks, we are a long way from the days when the House of Morgan was supposed to make the nation's economic decisions, at Broad and Wall. Our present social engineers find neither the charts of Adam Smith nor those of Karl Marx very useful. Both of these great observers wrote a century ago and more. Did we rely only on the findings of the 1830 physicists to make the bomb? New maps and charts must be drawn if we are to understand and effectively deal with the world of 1946. One useful distinction is between stimulating the economy indirectly through profits and savings, and stimulating it directly through wages and welfare outlays.

## The Trickle-Down Theory

Most people are now pretty well committed—at least in public—to the idea that the masses must buy a lot of goods if factories are to keep going, and business is to prosper. How can this be done most effectively? Discussion often brings out the "trickle-down" idea of progress, versus the mass purchasing power idea. Shall we encourage the rich, hoping that their gains will trickle down through the economic structure to fertilize all levels, or shall we put purchasing power directly into the hands of the people?

Oscar Gass recently summarized the two schools in these words.[1] For the first:

> Preserve profits and savings or you shall not have prosperity. With greatly unequal rewards as a stimulating force, the economy will progress so that all classes of the population will be wealthier than they would otherwise.

For the mass-purchasers:

> Maintain demand. Avoid idle resources. With comparative equality of income, consumption will be high, and even investment will be greater than in an economy where great inequalities of income lead to prolonged periods of unemployment.

A typical defender of the trickle-down theory doubts if full employment is possible in a "free" society, and vigorously rejects the idea of a mature economy. He is for low income taxes and a balanced budget—a paradox which he seldom attempts to explain. He appeals to history to bear him out that his is the American way.

1. *New Republic,* January 14, 1946.

The American idea in the past has often been to let a man get as rich as he pleased, and then count on him "to keep the money in circulation," to distribute libraries, memorial hospitals, and so on. In practice, however, this idea has been modified by large government subsidies to the mass of the people in the form of free land in the West, Civil War pensions, public schools. Sometimes profits and savings do really trickle down. Lately they have often dammed up in pools of idle money.[2]

## No Rigid Class Lines

Although the argument seems to follow the class struggle concept in a general way, closer examination shows this is not so. Big business is split wide open on the matter. Many managers believe that Henry Ford was on the right track when he made the mass purchasing of automobiles possible, along with a $5 minimum daily wage. The whole formula of big volume, high wages, low overhead per unit, low prices, has not been unacceptable to big business for a generation, and many companies have vigorously acted on it. During the 1920's it had a wide vogue, and even a title: "the economy of high wages." Trade papers of the decade were full of it.

This is a long way from the trickle-down theory. Indeed, it squares pretty generally with what Walter Reuther was fighting for in the General Motors strike—high wages, high production, low prices, good profits. Perhaps a majority of American tycoons are trickle-downers in their own hearts— certainly they would like to get their surtax rates down— but many run their corporations on the other policy.

2. As examined in detail in book 3 of this series, *Where's the Money Coming From?*

*A Massive Trend*

Ever since World War I, the march of events both here and abroad has tended to support the mass-purchase school, with the trickle-downers increasingly on the defensive. Perhaps the most significant example of the trend is the graduated income tax. In 1912 there was no federal income tax at all in this country. The law was finally passed after a ferocious battle as an item in President Wilson's New Freedom in 1913. The early rates would make you weep, they were so modest. *But the principle of graduation* was employed from the beginning—the bigger the income, the bigger the *rate.* By 1923, the top rate was up to 50 per cent for incomes of $5,000,000 and more.[3] By 1940, it was up to 75 per cent for $5,000,000 incomes, and 62 per cent for $200,000 incomes. In 1944, it was 91 per cent for all incomes above $200,000. In Britain, the largest possible take-home income during the war was about $25,000, and fewer than 200 individuals in the country received it.

All nations have been pruning it off at the top and plowing it in at the bottom, war or peace, always in the direction of equalization. The graduated income tax has displaced property taxes as the main revenue producer in modern societies.

It is not the only evidence, however, of the policy of building up the purchasing power of the masses. We have mentioned the Ford formula. Then there is modern advertising. Many selling campaigns have been keyed to expand mass distribution, and so bring goods to people who never had them before—all kinds of goods, from toothbrushes to television sets. These mass assaults on the consumer do not

3. During the war it had been higher.

wait for his income to trickle down from above. If he hasn't the cash, let him sign on the dotted line of an installment contract. Many industries are now so geared to selling folks on the other side of the tracks, that a lower wage level would drive them out of business.

## Welfare Outlays

The government has taken a hand in stimulating purchasing power, not only via the income tax, but by more direct action. Mass standards have been raised through such devices as the Social Security Acts, the GI Bill of Rights, the REA, public housing, the HOLC, the Minimum Wage Law, public works, the Food Stamp Plan—to name a few.

All over the world a similar movement is in evidence, except that it moves faster. Canada, following a score of other nations, has recently included "family allowances" in her social security system, whereby mothers get monthly checks from the government to care for their babies—the more babies the bigger the check. Nothing could be more direct than this!

Mr. Roosevelt was elected four times on the strength of his support of the mass-purchasing-power policy. Mr. Churchill was defeated after V-E Day because his party, while not opposed, was only lukewarm about it. Sir William Beveridge is a world-renowned champion of mass-purchasing via social security. France, Belgium, Norway, Holland, Italy, are all moving in the direction of equalization. So are Sweden, Australia, New Zealand, and many countries in Latin America.

It is difficult to see how anyone with a sense of history

and the power of objective analysis can believe that this massive planetary trend can be reversed. Suppose it is momentarily checked or diverted. Will the graduated income tax be permanently rescinded? Or social security laws? If the United States falls into another depression, will Congress refuse mass relief on the classical slogan of letting nature take her course? In short, will we, or will any other people committed to mass production ever go back to the practice of fertilizing chiefly from the top? More and more that once forgotten man, the consumer, takes the center of the stage.

If the mass of the people are prosperous everyone is prosperous, including the upper brackets. All the time that well-to-do citizens were bitterly criticizing the New Deal, their net worth was steadily increasing. If, however, the upper brackets are surfeited with funds while the lower brackets have none, there will be little demand for investment and plant expansion. Idle money will presently choke the whole economy, ruining rich along with poor. This seems to be the first law of social dynamics in the power age.

The real question before the country is not whether we are going to return to the gilded age of Astor, Vanderbilt and Morgan, with wages at a dollar a day. The question is whether we are going to wait for the welfare economy to come hit or miss, per Model A, or plan its coming intelligently.

### Features of Model B

Broadly speaking, there are two things to plan for in a well designed Middle Road program.

*First,* ways and means must be provided to smooth out

the business cycle, so that production, employment and confidence remain continuously high.

*Second,* certain essential services must be planned for, which otherwise would not be adequately furnished.

The first has to do with quantity, the second with quality. A full employment economy where citizens spent their labor manufacturing nothing but chewing gum and juke boxes would not be very successful.

Here is a list of some of the major items on the agenda for Model B. Observe this is not a planned economy as such. For the most part it is simply a continuation of what has been developing in this country for many years.

1. A series of compensatory financial devices for smoothing out the business cycle and halting both inflation and depression. These devices include a full employment bill like S.380, incentive taxation, public works, control of foreign trade and investment, the adjustment of income tax rates and social security tax rates, and adjustment of the national debt to help stabilize the economy.[4] It is interesting to note that $10 billion of our debt was actually retired in early 1946, reducing the total from $280 billions to $270 billions—more than Secretary Mellon ever paid off at the height of the prosperous 1920's. Such debt-reduction at the upper arc of the cycle is a direct attack on inflation.

2. A flexible double budget, such as Sweden uses, where self-liquidating projects are kept out of the expenditure side, and capital outlays are properly amortized over the life of the asset. The present U.S. budget violates nearly every law of business and common sense, and tells us al-

---

4. See *Where's the Money Coming From?* for a detailed description of a compensatory economy.

most nothing meaningful about the state of the national finances. It has been a kind of golden calf to be worshipped, not a functional piece of machinery to be used for stabilizing the economy. Here we need a brand new mechanism.

3. Social security for every American, including unemployment insurance, old-age allowances, health insurance, aid for the handicapped and the blind.

4. The GI Bill of Rights for veterans, with especial consideration for disabled veterans.

5. Minimum wage and maximum hour legislation, to put a firm base under the whole economy.

6. Housing for everyone. Government subsidies for families which cannot afford decent, sanitary houses in which to bring up children. Heretofore, housing has been a prime example of the trickle-down theory. People in the lower brackets have mostly lived in somebody's old house.

7. Long-range conservation programs to hold the soils, waters, resources of America at par. Multiple-purpose dam projects and TVA developments come under this head. So do stock piles for critical resources.

8. A practical formula for keeping strikes and lockouts at a minimum. (Charles E. Wilson, of the General Electric Company, once proposed the price level of 1940, and the take-home pay of 1944 as necessary for full employment.[5]) Such a formula should include permanent labor-management committees as in wartime; something like the TWI war program for foremen and workers;[6] comprehensive conciliation and arbitration machinery; some recognized relationships between wages, output, prices and profits. We

5. Speech to Utility Executives, Atlanta, October 1944.
6. See this author's *Men at Work* (Harcourt, Brace) for description of these programs, especially Job Relations.

have forerunners in the Ford idea, in the collective bargaining of the men's clothing industry. It would be desirable to have collective bargaining handle the whole show, but this is not possible yet. Many of the unions are too green. The government will have to help in setting up the formula. It may have to fix some prices and some wage rates, as at present.

9. Perhaps the most important item in the whole agenda should be government aid for scientific research. Most American scientists want the National Science Foundation bills to pass Congress. They want to see the federal government help scientists to develop not only atomic research, but the peacetime uses of the proximity fuse, rocket ships, microbiology; the exploration of the ionosphere; the control of disease. Even more urgent in my opinion is an intensive stimulation of the social sciences, to help them begin to catch up with the runaway physical sciences.

Research is a kind of public works program so far as the economic effect is concerned, a modern and an effective kind. We should never spend another thin dime in leaf raking, as long as research projects are briefed and ready to be tackled. Many studies, of course, would be maintained on a continuous basis, but others could be held for employment projects when they should be needed.

10. Mounting guard over all these proposals should be a Stabilization Board composed of qualified experts, exceedingly well paid, who would set up instruments to record what was happening in the economy, just as scientists are setting up instruments to record the effects of the atomic bomb on naval vessels in the Marshall Islands. Findings and suggestions of this Board should be made available to

the public, to the President and to Congress, for action.[7]
The functions of the Board would include such matters as:

A reliable monthly count of the unemployed.

Regular and reliable estimates of gross national product and net national income.

A running inventory of natural resources.

A running inventory of new investment.

Close cooperation with the National Science Foundation in all major research projects.

Close cooperation with the UNO, the International Fund and the Bank. A running inventory of foreign commerce.

The coordination of all economic statistics in government agencies.

Specific suggestions for compensatory action in smoothing out the business cycle.

## Reforming Congress

These ten features of U.S. Model B will not help much without *improved machinery to make Congress work*. Congress is the heart of the democratic process. Every one of the items on the above agenda depends at some point on legislation. Yet as I write Congress has virtually ceased to function. It has discarded most of President Truman's program and offered nothing in its place. The Senate, recently fighting the FEPC with a filibuster—probably the most inane parliamentary device ever practiced—might as well have been on the moon for all the good it did us. If the representative form of government, says Thomas K. Finletter, "is unable to achieve what the people want, it may be repudiated and some other kind of government substituted for it."[8]

The chief effect of our political machinery is often to thwart the will of the people. In 27 out of the 79 Congresses

7. The Full Employment Bill as finally passed contains the rudiments of such a board.

8. *Can Representative Government Do the Job?* Reynal and Hitchcock, New York, 1945.

since 1788, at least one house of Congress has been of a different party from the President. A more exquisite method for smothering action is difficult to imagine. Even when Congress is of the same party, as at present, it often blocks the executive. No President ever started on better terms with Congress than ex-Senator Truman. The necessity for action forced him into an attempt at leadership, in which he of all men needed strong support. Did he get it from Congress? No indeed; his honeymoon was over in about six months. Today there is war to the death between the legislative and executive—proving, I think, that it isn't so much the men, it's the machinery.

The machinery set up by the founding fathers, and tinkered with considerably since, has come to look like a Rube Goldberg cartoon. Our British critics see it more objectively than we can. The London *Economist*,[9] analyzing our constitutional procedure, suggests that its lack of efficiency arises first from a distrust of all government as such; and second from fear that the federal government will encroach on the rights of the states. Great power is intentionally put in the hands of minorities—as in the case of the filibuster, where a handful of senators, if they have the lung capacity, can paralyze the whole federal organism.

"The American Constitution was deliberately designed," says the *Economist*, "to make it difficult for anybody to do anything." There is a premium on opposition—twenty chances of saying no to every one of saying yes. Only a very great leader, a Lincoln, Wilson, or a Roosevelt, can surmount the checks and balances, and really lead the people.

In 1944, the Chairman of the vitally important Appropriations Committee in the Senate was 86 years old. The

9. May 17, 1941.

Chairman of the Agricultural Committee, 80; of Commerce, 71; of Reclamation, 71; of Naval Affairs, 71; of Post Offices, 75; of Privileges and Election, 77. The Chairman of the puissant Foreign Affairs Committee in the House was 74; of Rules, 78; of Ways and Means, 78. . . . This situation has been called Gerontocracy—government by old men.

In March 1946, Congress received from its own committee, from Senator La Follette and Representative Monroney, a far-reaching plan of reorganization. This has a better chance of getting attention than any outsider's plan, such as Mr. Finletter's, or that of the National Planning Association. It called for a reduction of the Senate's 33 standing committees to 16, and of those of the House from 48 to 18. It called for the regulation of lobbyists, for more research aid to overworked Congressmen, for better pay and more security, and improved liaison between House and Senate, and between Congress and the White House. It did not advocate the end of Gerontocracy, but you can't get everything at once.

If the nation can repair its political machinery so that it is capable of getting things done when they must be done in this atomic age, the outlook on the home front brightens. The agenda for Model B can be put through, if the people really mean what they say in the polls of public opinion. Veterans and the rest of us ought to be able to get the continuity of employment and economic security we crave. We ought to get them along the Middle Road, without the authoritarian state, indeed with a good deal less government interference than during the war.

Model B, however, will not be brought by gremlins. We shall have to go out and fight for it.

# 11

# $E = MC^2$

DURING THE WAR, scientists developed 2–4–D for the extermination of weeds, DDT for insects, 1080 for rats, and $E=MC^2$ for men.

Professor Einstein gave us the last in his theory of relativity forty years ago, but it remained for the Manhattan Project to demonstrate the complete reliability of the formula. "E" stands for energy in kilowatt hours, "M" for mass in kilograms, "C" is the speed of light—186,000 miles a second, as you know,[1] the square of which makes a very tidy sum. When a chain reaction is set up in M, the resulting energy released becomes something which only the survivors of Hiroshima and Nagasaki can adequately report on.

Furthermore, these chains were *not* carried all the way out per formula. The fission effect stopped relatively early in Japan. Already, it is said, atomic bombs have been produced which are a great many times as destructive. Already New York could be ripped apart from the Battery to Central Park in one shuddering cataclysm.

1. Neatly verified again by the 2.4 seconds it took to bounce a radar beam off the moon. Radar travels at the speed of light.

## The Third Landmark

So mankind comes to its third, and perhaps its last great landmark—something to make the models we were discussing in the preceding chapters look relatively minor. The discovery of fire, the development of agriculture, the release of atomic power—and after some thousands of years the creature called man has either mastered his environment or caused it to destroy him.

In the late Tertiary epoch, 7,000,000 to 1,000,000 B.C., anthropoid apes roamed over Asia, Europe and Africa, some of them rather man-like.[2] One branch in Asia finally came down out of the trees and began walking erect. It had a big brain for an ape, and of course an opposed thumb with which to manipulate things—sticks, axes, some day cyclotrons.

In the Lower Paleolithic epoch, 1,000,000 to 50,000 B.C., this creature invented fire, and became radically progressive in the reduction of the weight of its skull and jaws. In due course a race evolved not far different from the Australian bushmen of today. Fist axes, choppers, and other crude tools were made from flaked stone. Hunting was the chief economic occupation. The brain case grew larger. Language probably developed along with the first tools. One needs to explain to one's fellows how to use a tool—a thing no ape can do.

The Upper Paleolithic, 50,000 to 10,000 B.C., brought a great advance in stone-working. Experts could strike off a long, fine flake from a core and out of it make knives, arrowheads, spear points, files, awls, scrapers, with which

2. Following William Howells, *Mankind So Far,* Doubleday, Doran, New York, 1944.

to work wood, skin, and bone. Later came the dog and the bow and arrow; then canoes, netting, basketry. Modern Eskimos, where uncorrupted by the white man, live a life similar to the Upper Paleolithic. It was still a hunting and fishing culture, with a world population, Howells estimates, of not more than 10,000,000. That was about all the environment could support.

The Neolithic Age, beginning on the Persian plateau around 10,000 B.C., inaugurated the *second* great revolution in the history of *homo sapiens*. First he came down from the trees and discovered fire; now he discovered how to domesticate plants and animals. For the first time a settled community became possible. No longer was it necessary to follow the migrations of wild animals for one's food. People could hoe a garden with a forked stick, milk a goat, and stay put. It is impossible to over-emphasize the importance of this progression.

With the Bronze Age, about 5,000 B.C., a pair of oxen yoked to a metal plow could so improve the efficiency of bread production, that a small percentage of mankind could be permanently released from the fields, and cities became possible. The first city we know of was Harappa in India; then Ur and Kish in Mesopotamia; Thebes, Karnak, the cities of ancient Crete, and so to Troy, Sparta, Corinth and Athens. With the cities came kings to rule over them, priests to pray for them, artisans and silversmiths who never laid hand to a plow; markets, trade routes, galleys, prostitutes, pyramids, temples, tenements, and slums—and most important of all, writing, mathematics, and the concept of science.

By A.D. 1600, the population of the world had increased

to perhaps 400 million, and Galileo laid down first principles for the machine age. By the time the atomic bomb was dropped, population had increased fivefold to two billion. This growth was made possible by inanimate energy and the factory system, together with the control of communicable diseases. To go back now to the Paleolithic Age would cost the lives of perhaps ninety-five out of every one hundred living persons.

The destruction of Hiroshima on August 6, 1945, marked the third great epoch in the history of mankind. The way now lies open to the pulverizing of all cities, everywhere.[3] The way also lies open to unprecedented increases in production, living standards, public health.

Dr. Howells does not believe that man will entirely destroy himself through cataclysm—but he wrote before the bomb. *Homo sapiens,* he says, is one of the toughest, most tenacious, most adaptable of all the animals. He is still largely unspecialized for a given environment, which is a great advantage, as compared with highly specialized animals, like the giraffe or the anteater. But even man could hardly adapt himself to perpetual explosions.

What the bomb does is to threaten our cities, and thus printing, science, the humanities. People would no longer have time to think. Atomic fission, unless it wipes out all land life, will not entirely destroy man; it will just pitch him back 100,000 years or so into the Paleolithic. As we have seen, it is quite a haul up from there. . . . Sometimes one wonders if we ever went through the cycle before.

3. See final report of General H. H. Arnold, *The New York Times,* August 18, ₵945. Also testimony of Philip Morrison before Senate Committee, *New Republic,* February 11, 1946.

## The First Reaction

A survey of newspaper editorials and front-page comment the week of August 11, 1945, showed the bomb had touched off the following reactions:[4]

Relief that the war was ending.
Relief that we had developed the bomb before Germany did.
Question: Can social thinking catch up with physical science?
War is now too terrible to be endured.
The need for a workable world organization becomes imperative.
The peacetime possibilities of atomic energy excite speculation.

In the discussion after August 6 the fifth reaction seemed practically unanimous: that the bomb had made some sort of a world state mandatory.[5] Most citizens appeared willing to surrender large segments of American sovereignty. Most, I believe, still are. The idea that the bell tolls for all of us made impressive gains.

With people all over the world in this frame of mind, the outlook for peace is distinctly brighter. If war should come, however, the outlook for one stone standing on another is distinctly darker. The major problem, as I see it, *is whether the present leaders of mankind, especially those of the Big Three nations, can really grasp the significance of atomic fission.* Back of the leaders, people everywhere should be putting on constant pressure for appropriate action. Both leaders and people should feel the urgency in the pit of their stomachs. No Congressman should ever be permitted to open his mail in the morning without finding several postcards inscribed "$E=MC^2$—What are *you* doing about it?"

The problem is really one for the social scientists. I do

4. Prepared by Twohey Analysis of Newspaper Opinion.
5. See, for instance, the great success of Emery Reves' book, *The Anatomy of Peace*, Harper, New York, 1945.

not mean they are now equal to solving it; I mean, as George Lundberg says, nobody else can. Thus it is a race with time—as indeed the Manhattan Project itself was. Meanwhile, until the social scientists and the rest of us are really aware of this third great landmark, we cannot even begin to cope with its problems.

### To Make Us Aware

The physical world has a certain structure. The physical scientists have now learned to understand it—not completely, but enough to tear the fundamental building blocks apart. They have done this by a vast project of planned cooperative research, covering five years and costing two billions. The world's political and industrial leaders are not scientists; most of them never went beyond simple algebra. But it is of the utmost importance that they respect and understand in a broad way what the scientists have done. Otherwise we are led by men who do not know the shape of the world they are trying to lead, or the forces now loose within it.

Not only must leaders exercise their brains to an unwonted degree, they must exercise their imaginations. They have got to see the unearthly glare, feel the shattering crunch as energy is released in these magnitudes. That mushroom of cumulus smoke in the stratosphere must be ever before their eyes. They must see, hear, smell, feel— almost taste—a chain reaction; it should be etched forever in the nervous system.

If the bomb is considered as just another element in power politics, just another military weapon, only stronger, the Paleolithic Age surely awaits us. Atomic fission simply is not that kind of event. Our leaders must come to see it in its true dimension, a blinding, shattering force, ranking with the discovery of fire, and the discovery of agriculture. In such perspective they may be able to deal with it.

## Continuous Exhibit

It has been proposed that the United Nations Assembly be taken *en masse* to watch the U.S. Navy's test of the bomb in the Marshall Islands.[6] This is a move in the right direction. We never learn from words, speeches, books, *by themselves*. A human being must first experience light rays, sound waves, sensations striking his nervous system, before he can speak or think intelligently about the things to which the sensations refer. From this direct contact, his whole mental world is built up. After enough contacts, words and books can become meaningful.

Most scientists keep this direct contact. Academic scholars often do not. Many of them labor under a punishing handicap of abstract words unconnected with space-time events. The philosophies and the dialectics go round and round without hitting anything. The great strength of the scientists is that they admit their talk is meaningless, and their conclusions invalid, unless these can pass the test of physical experiment. If the results are positive, the talk makes sense. Galileo broke up two thousand years of portico philosophy —where it was argued that heavy bodies fall faster than light bodies—by dropping light and heavy shot from the Leaning Tower of Pisa and timing the fall. The experiment showed they arrived simultaneously.

6. The real test, I am told, will be the explosion under water, planned for 1947.

*Why Not All Leaders?*

Why not carry the idea of first-hand experience much further? Why not expose *all* the outstanding leaders of the world to direct chain reaction? Why not summon every Congressman, the heads of government departments, governors of states, university presidents, important tycoons, the executive committees of the AF of L, the CIO, the Farm Bureau Federation, the veterans' organizations, and plenty of school teachers? Why not have the British Parliament and Cabinet, and the Supreme Council of the USSR? Why not have the Pope, the Grand Mullah, Gandhi, a panel of bishops, the chiefs of state of all the nations, and all the admirals and generals who carry real weight?

Let them stand there and watch: If a few get a little too near and are knocked over—like those extra-curious scientists in the New Mexico desert—that is all right, too. Protect them from lethal rays, but let them get knocked over. That is what they came for.

Furthermore there should be a regular exhibit, say every six months, staged by the United Nations, in the Sahara, the Gobi, Death Valley, and other desert areas of the world. No person should be elected or appointed to high office, anywhere, without having had at least one first-hand encounter with the event corresponding to $E = MC^2$.

Many of our leaders have had legal training. Thomas Reed Powell, of the Harvard Law School, once observed: "If you think that you can think about a thing, firmly attached to something else, without thinking of the thing it is attached to, then you have a legal mind." One would feel safer if leaders had to pass an examination in simple mathematics, in distinguishing clearly between a fact and a generalization, in the scientific attitude—and so avoid that verbal habit mentioned earlier, of leaping from an unwarranted assumption to a foregone conclusion.

If it turns out too much to ask a Congressman to demonstrate his ability to move logically from cause to effect, then we had better draw our Congressmen from a different panel. A politician is *not* a scientist, and no one should ask him to be—at least until the social sciences have developed much further. But in the atomic age he should be acquainted with the scientific method, and should know which way the scientists are steering the human race. He should realize what complex cause-and-effect relationships exist in human affairs, and the resulting difficulty of control.

## Rank and File

For those of us who are not top leaders, for the rank and file of literate humanity, the schools and press should place far more emphasis on mathematics, logic, semantics, straight thinking, and the scientific attitude. How many of us can state clearly what constitutes a controlled experiment? Small children begin by thinking pretty straight, because of their first-hand experience with a bumpy world. Later they are deluged with high-order abstractions, and their pristine approach to the laws of cause and effect is corrupted.

All of us, children as well as adults, furthermore, should see such moving pictures or stills of Hiroshima and Nagasaki as are available, from either American or Japanese sources. We should see the dead, the wounded, the smashed hospitals, the agony.[7] They should be run in every theatre

7. See, for instance, the Catholic Father's terrible story in *Time,* February 11, 1946.

in the world at regular intervals, without soft music, without announcers who coat their vocal chords with honey. We should take these horrors straight, hard, and unvarnished. If anybody faints, that is all right too. Movies are not as good as seeing the real thing, but they get into the nervous system after a fashion, and leave a sharper imprint, for most people, than words can ever do. Thomas A. Edison used to say the shortest route to the intelligence runs over the optic nerve.

All theatres should also show documentary films of the Navy tests, and of all future chain reactions in bombs. Then there should be frequent documentaries of the development of atomic energy, with moving diagrams tracing the principles involved, so far as they can be simplified. We should see the uranium mines, the piles, the shields, the new power units; we should see medical diagnosis by virtue of the new rays, cancer research, heat therapy—all the good and cheerful aspects of nuclear fission. We should be taught what inspection means.

Talk, editorials, columns, dissertations like the one I am writing, are not going to help much. The words are already wearing thin. We must constantly be *shocked* into awareness—as when lightning strikes close by. Only first-hand experience can hold us to the task of saving our civilization. If the social scientists can refine and sharpen this approach, the world will be profoundly grateful. But they can do more than this. Social scientists can help leaders draft the machinery to control the bomb. They can help break up the unfounded notion that man has an instinct for war. He has a pugnacious instinct, which is very different.[8] War is a cold-

8. Julian Huxley in *The New York Times Magazine*, February 10, 1946.

blooded business of organization. Look at the Pentagon Building.

A woman's magazine has listed the ways in which many people are beginning to escape from this discipline.[9]

Let's not talk about it.
The higher-ups will solve it.
A defense will be found; it always has.
They won't dare use it.
The U.S. can stay ahead of all enemies.
Anyway, we're keeping it secret.
We've never lost a war.
We all have to die sometime.
You can't change human nature.
I'll be dead by then.
We ought to bottle up those scientists.

The idea I advocate is to shut off these infantile escapes, and try to look our destiny in the face.


Sooner or later this moment had to come. It has been inevitable since mankind came down from trees and shaped the first fist axe. *Homo sapiens* is the kind of animal which was bound to be curious about the structure of the world around him. Now he has found the answer, or a large part of it.

Has he found it too soon? This is a meaningless question. Nobody knows, or can know, whether it is too soon, until the proposition has been demonstrated. If a handful of us wake up some stormy morning to find ourselves in the Lower Paleolithic, we can conclude it was too soon. Until then, it is our duty to try and meet the challenge.

If enough of us can become aware of what has happened in this third great technical landmark in history, we may be

9. Marjorie Laurence Street in *Ladies' Home Journal*, February 1946.

able to force our leaders to accept a piece of international machinery adequate to contain Einstein's equation. Technical controls will be needed to protect us in the years it will take to devise trustworthy political controls. The physical scientists, who are showing the most gratifying terror of what they have done, can assist with such plans. The first *political* problem is to get the rest of us as intelligently terrified as the scientists. Then we will keep on pushing until an appropriate solution is found. Here is a goal to challenge all our energies!

### To Contain the Equation

The first real hope of controlling $E=MC^2$ came with the publication in April 1946 of a report prepared for Dean Acheson of the State Department by a special committee under David Lilienthal. The report sets forth these propositions:[10]

1. An agreement between nations to forego atomic weapons will not provide security. This is unpleasant but true.
2. An international inspection system attempting to ferret out violations of such agreement will probably not work.
3. Uranium is the only known element which can maintain a chain reaction.
4. With uranium available, bombs can be produced by any nation having the requisite scientific staff.
5. "Denatured" fissionable materials can also be produced from uranium. These are suitable for peacetime uses, will not explode, and cannot be converted into bombs except in large industrial developments which should be easy to see, and would take a year or two to build.

10. A Report on the International Control of Atomic Energy. Superintendent of Documents, Washington, 1946. In June 1946, Mr. Baruch used part of the report in the official policy of the U.S.

6. The United States now has a monopoly of atomic bombs but cannot hope to maintain it for long.

On the basis of the above facts, the committee proposes to set up an international Atomic Development Authority which would:

1. Control and operate all uranium deposits and refineries located anywhere in the world.
2. Produce fissionable materials therefrom.
3. Lease "denatured" fissionable materials to nations for peacetime uses, under license and reasonable terms of inspection.
4. Carry on further research in the field of atomic energy.

Here at last is a plan that attacks the problem from the technical end, and sets about constructing a monopoly as efficient as some of our international commodity agreements. That the authors are aware of political implications as well is shown in these words of Harry A. Winne, a member of the committee: "With a plan of international control of atomic energy effectively in operation, we shall know what other nations are doing. Without such a plan, we shall fear what they are doing, and the fear will grow, and grow, and grow."

The plan needs to be adopted promptly, through the initiative of the United States, before the horrors spread any farther from the Pandora's box which was opened on August 6. With its adoption, power politics will be disarmed. An effective beginning will be made toward the world state.

Then Jeff and his comrades will not have fought and died in vain.